Patterns
of Destiny

Patterns of Destiny

by Hans Holzer

Nash Publishing, Los Angeles

Library of Congress Catalog Card Number: 73-83535
International Standard Book Number: 0-8402-1323-9

Published simultaneously in the United States and Canada
by Nash Publishing Corporation, 9255 Sunset Boulevard
Los Angeles, California 90069

Printed in the United States of America

First Printing

In memory of my parents.

Contents

Introduction

Common expressions such as, "you only live once," and "this is the only life you have—enjoy it," and "you come this way only once" are good indications that the average person considers life to be a unique and fleeting experience. Consequently, the fact that life is comparatively short and ends inevitably in death has given people an excuse to live a life of material enjoyment. In all civilizations and at all times there were those who used this fundamental view of human life as an excuse to indulge in excesses in the enjoyment of the physical pleasures of this world. To persuade them that their hedonistic approach to life was not necessarily the best one, and to consider spiritual values as well, required a powerful counter-argument. This counter-argument became the focal rallying point of establishment religion. Only by promising man a better life in the hereafter or resurrection at some vaguely defined future time, could religion hope to impress man with the need for a balanced philosophy of life in which the material and the spiritual balanced and offset each other. Religion tried by persuasion and, when persuasion failed, by threats: the threat of punishment once the sinner crosses the threshold of death and finds himself in a world divided between heaven and hell, and the reward of a blissful perennial state of happiness called heaven in which the devout could dwell forever as a reward for restraint while on earth.

But even from the very beginning there runs a motif of reincarnation through all religious faiths; in the West belief in reincarnation was part and parcel of the Old Religion, later known as Anglo-Saxon or Celtic witchcraft, and in the East it still furnishes one of the principal rallying points of the Buddhist faith and of certain other religious sects partially derived from Buddhist principles, such as Tibetan Lamaism. In the Western tradition based on Christianity the belief in reincarnation was present at the very beginning. There are numerous references in the Old and New Testaments, pointing to a belief in reincarnation. Of this more later. Only in recent years has the scientific exploration of experiences pointing towards the existence of reincarnation been pursued. Until the latter part of the nineteenth century, psychical research was in the hands of amateurs or at times quacks; with the emergence of an ordered scientific approach to the phenomena of human personality nowadays classified as ESP phenomena, the subject of reincarnation was also dealt with. Today, after a hiatus of perhaps fifty years, the subject of reincarnation is again a very current one, because it seems to answer so many questions left unanswered by both science and establishment religion. Particularly among the young, the cries for information on previous and future lives is very loud, for it does furnish them with an explanation for the many injustices they see all around. Consequently, some scholars have not feared to tread where others might, and have gone on record saying that reincarnation seems factual to them. Foremost amongst those who have put their scientific acumen on the side that favors reincarnation is Dr. Ian Stevenson, School of Medicine, University of Virginia, Charlottesville. Dr. Banerjee has done similar work in India. In an earlier book of mine entitled *Born Again* I described a number of compelling cases proving that the evidence for reincarnation can be both detailed and factual.

The purpose of this work is to acquaint my readers with new and unpublished material pointing in the direction of reincarnation, and to analyze this material in terms of some sort of system that would allow us to understand the phenomenon better than we have in the past. Furthermore, it is my intention to delineate a system under which reincarnation and karma seem to work. The purpose of this is to allow my readers to come to some conclusion concerning their philosophy of life; for it is my contention that the system involving reincarnation and the karmic law is the only plausible explanation for our world, the universe of which it is part, and the seeming contradictions found therein. *Patterns Of Destiny* is intended both as a practical handbook for those interested in reincarnation, their own as well as that of others, and as a scientific report on recent and well-researched cases tending to prove my contention that reincarnation is a fact, and a fact for everyone.

PART ONE

Chapter 1
Déjà vu and Recurrent Dreams

Almost everybody has at one time or another had a sudden, short experience called déjà vu—a distinct feeling that one has done something before, has been to a place before, or heard something said before that is now being enacted. Logical thinking tells one that this cannot be so because the event is just taking place, but there is a very strong feeling nevertheless that the scene one is just experiencing has been experienced before. This is generally followed by a nagging doubt as to whether one is correct about the situation at the same time that there is a certainty that one is familiar with what is being said or done at that precise moment. Orthodox psychologists and psychiatrists have long explained this as a trick of memory. They say that people sometimes open a "false memory door" and thus experience a feeling of previous knowledge when in fact there is no such knowledge. But the same psychiatrists failed to tell us how the mind accomplishes this marvelous trick of "false memory doors." In this case the commonly heard explanation for déjà vu is simply not sufficient. Déjà vu means "already seen" in French, but it covers experiences of "already heard" and "already known" as well. Foreknowledge without a logical base might be a better way of describing this phenomenon.

3

Hardly anyone goes through life without having at least one or more such experiences. They are probably among the most common forms of ESP phenomena. Undoubtedly, the majority of these déjà vu experiences can be explained on the basis of precognition. An experience is foreseen and not noted at the time. Later, when the experience becomes objective reality and one goes through it, one suddenly remembers "as if in a flash" that one has had knowledge of this particular experience before. In other words, the majority of déjà vu experiences are nothing more than forgotten precognitive incidents. However, there is a residue of such experiences which cannot be explained on this basis. Among them are such cases as people coming to a town or a house for the first time and having exact foreknowledge of what the house or town looks like, even to the point of knowing specific rooms, furniture, and arrangements in rooms and other details that are far beyond the scope of ordinary precognition. There is a thin line where the precognitive experience must end; precognitive experiences do not contain exhaustive details, including names, dates, arrangements in rooms, etc., to the point where the details are so specific and so numerous that only a person who would have been familiar with the arrangements could have remembered them. In general, precognitive experiences are partial and stress certain salient points, a few details perhaps, but never the entire picture. When the number of remembered details becomes very large we must always suspect reincarnative memories.

I have reported on a number of such cases in my previous book dealing with the subject, *Born Again*. A young man in upstate New York went to a house he had never been to before in his lifetime. Upon arrival he became very excited and suddenly remembered every detail about the house he was about to enter. When he reached the upper story, he told his companions what lay around the corner and what the room to which they would next come would look like. All this was confirmed. Had this merely been a precognitive experience, he would have had a flash of himself coming to this house, seeing himself enter it, but the foreknowledge of details would have been absent.

It would be erroneous to assume that all such déjà vu experiences have deeper significance, or that they even represent important memories. Quite the opposite is true; the majority of such remembrances seem to be everyday details of no particular significance. They are, however, important in an indirect way; by heaping a number of commonplace memories one upon the other, a continual basis for remembering is established. As with all other psychic experiences, there is always an emotional base present. Purely logical or mechanical details are never remembered. Similar to the déjà vu experience in the waking state is the recurrent dream. Since man's unconscious mind can be entered more easily during the sleeping state, a large number of psychic experiences take place while the individual is asleep. It appears that the communications, such as they may be, can be implanted in the unconscious of the sleeper with less resistance from the conscious mind than would be the case if the communication were attempted during a wakeful state.

The majority of dreams, however, do not fall into this category. There are four different types of dreams. The first type of dream may be caused by physical discomfort; the second type may contain suppressed emotional material, frequently of a symbolic nature and furnishing the basic material for the psychoanalyst; a third type of dream contains psychic material if the individual is sufficiently advanced in his or her ESP development; and the fourth type of dream corresponds to what is now called "out of the body" experience in which the etheric body of the individual travels to places outside of the physical body. Recurrent dreams fall into the third category and consist of precise, frequently emotionally tinged dreams

5

which repeat identical or very similar scenes more than one time. The more frequently the recurrent dream occurs, the stronger the emotional memory seems to be. This does not mean that potential reincarnation material cannot also be found in single dreams; but recurrent dreams are inevitably connected with some sort of reincarnation remembrance. In the recurrent-dream phenomenon the dream is usually well remembered on awakening, to the point that it is hard to shake even during the course of the day. When it reoccurs it is usually identical with previous incidents and in some cases may advance the action, as it were, of the previous dream, generally slightly, but significantly.

Probably the most revealing case of recurrent dreams involving reincarnation memories was published by me in *Born Again* and involved Pat Wollenberg of Illinois, who remembered significant data about a previous lifetime in Scotland in the early sixteen-hundreds. If it were not for her recurrent dream memories, communicated to me at the time, subsequent research would not have been undertaken and additional material would not have been uncovered.

It is the nature of dreams to be condensed versions of actual occurrences. Consequently, we find that even ordinary dreams are very short representations of what under ordinary logical conditions would be extended periods of time. In the recurrent dream episodes the number of facts pertaining to a given situation are also strongly condensed, that is to say, only the key words or facts are flashed into the unconscious mind of the sleeper, much in the nature of a telegram. On awakening, the key words are easily remembered and can be written down, if necessary, in order to be followed up. Recurrent dreams are generally very emotional, frequently deal with situations involving death or tragedy or, at the very least, highly dramatic conditions. It is also significant that the dreamer always sees himself or herself in the dream, not as an outsider but as a participant. If the physical figure of the sleeper is not actually perceived, a sense of presence is nevertheless felt.

In this respect recurrent dreams differ greatly from ordinary psychic experiences, even those that may be ascribed to intervention from deceased individuals trying to communicate with the sleeper and using the sleeper as a medium for their unexpressed communications. This is an important point since those not too familiar with reincarnation research but otherwise cognizant of ESP and psychic phenomena tend to substitute ordinary ESP communications for genuine reincarnation explanations. The difference between a psychic experience where the sleeper merely acts as the *receiver* of information from a deceased individual and those where the sleeper is himself involved as a *principal,* is very important: In recurrent dreams containing reincarnation material the sleeper sees himself or feels himself in the scene. Where the sleeper merely acts as medium, he never puts himself into the scene but feels, very probably, that he is only an observer, standing on the outside, as it were, looking in.

The people to whom events of this kind happen come from all walks of life, all social backgrounds and are of varying ages. There is nothing specific about them, nothing that would single them out as being prone to reincarnation memories or even to psychic phenomena. Having ESP or experiencing something along psychic lines is in no way unnatural or supernatural and people who partake of these experiences can be any kind of people, you and me included.

Diane Rogers is in her early forties, a Chicago housewife and mother, and works as a film laboratory technician. Her husband is a supervisor for Swift, and she has two children, age ten and fifteen. When she first contacted me, it was because reincarnation memories and other psychic experiences had disturbed her.

7

She wanted to know what they meant and if necessary how to cope with them. Her interest in the occult was practically nonexistent at first, and she had only once before been hypnotized, three years prior to our meeting, when she wanted to stop smoking.

When we met at the Hampshire House in Chicago, she was visibly nervous. Her face was pale. She smoked one cigarette after another, since the attempt to stop smoking had evidently not been a success. "I have had numerous dreams and feelings and most of them involve my husband or close friends," she explained. "One dream involved my husband and another woman, and in it I actually saw them on the street in front of a restaurant in the town where I was then living, Harvey, Illinois. Her face was not clear, but on her sweater was the initial J. In the dream I was very upset and I remember stamping on my husband's foot and kicking him in the shin and then walking away. A few days later I learned through a friend that my husband had indeed had an affair with a young lady whose initial was J. She worked in the restaurant I had seen in my dream. I confronted him with the evidence of the dream and he admitted it. But he wanted to know how I knew about it." Telling her husband that she had dreamed the information would not have done any good so she simply told him that a friend had given her the information. Since Miss Rogers had expressed a desire to be regressed hypnotically in order to learn about any previous lives, I wondered whether she had ever had any indication that she had lived before.

"I've always had a strong interest in the pre-Civil War South," she explained. "I read everything and anything I can get my hands on and I am very interested in the period, but only until the middle of the war, and then I don't seem to care any longer. Coming back from Florida in 1968 I was going through Georgia and admiring the countryside. My father-in-law was driving and

8

we were just passing through a wooded area. Suddenly I had a strong impulse to go down a certain side road, but I am sure if I had gone down that road I would have discovered something about a previous life in Georgia. I have a feeling that I lived as a slave."

"Have you ever had any specific dreams in which you saw yourself as someone selse?" I inquired.

"I've seen myself wearing long dresses but I couldn't see the face, just the clothes. I've seen myself drowning, it is always dark in those dreams, and it seems to have something to do with a wooden bridge. I have a recurrent dream about being in the water and it being dark."

Mary Chappel is the youngest of four children of a dairyman; she lived in Missouri for twelve years before moving to California. Now thirty-eight years old and married, she has six children, three boys and three girls, and lives in a small town in the San Francisco Bay area. Mrs. Chappel has had various ESP experiences throughout most of her adult life. On June 9, 1970 she and her daughter Linda Gail were on a shopping expedition to the nearby town of Vallejo. Somehow she felt the urge to go back home by way of Sonoma where there are a number of historical landmarks. They decided to stop at the old San Francisco Solarno Mission and tour it, especially General Vallejo's home. They followed the directions leading there:

"The oddest feeling came over us as soon as we got out of the car," Mrs Chappel explained, "a feeling that we had been there before, but of course neither of us ever had. As we walked through the gardens and the house we could sense someone right at our shoulders, but no one was to be seen. It wasn't a scary feeling but a warm feeling as if someone were saying, 'Welcome back, where have you been?' " Mrs. Chappel then continues her account: "The objects in the room seemed familiar, especially a piano in the living room and one of the upstairs bedrooms. It was all we could do to drag ourselves away, but we felt a pull back for months. Finally, we were able to go back on October 18, 1971. The feelings were stronger than ever, in fact, we even had tears in our eyes, tears of joy at being there again.

"While on this same trip we stopped at the Petaluma Adobe near Santa Rosa, another place that had belonged to General Vallejo. The same feeling of being home hit us and we knew what was in some of the rooms before looking in at the doors. While walking on the upstairs balcony, the years seemed to melt away and we could sense how things had been a hundred years before. Also, throughout the hour we were there, we could smell flowers in bloom although it was mid-October and there were no flowers around." Salvador Vallejo was a young officer in the Mexican army serving in California. In 1833 he was sent to inspect Russian activities at Fort Ross near Bodega Bay. Eventually the region became part of the United States with the blessing and the advice of General Vallejo.

Karen Massey contacted me in New York because of what seemed to her a puzzling experience. Consequently I met with her in October 1972 when I visited Houston, Texas. The attractive young woman had had some premonitory dreams most of her growing years. About five years ago, she began to feel that she really belonged in the France of about 1740. She kept seeing herself dressed in long fluffy dresses. In another scene she saw herself in what she considers the early eighteen-hundreds, somewhere in an area that had not been fully settled as yet. She and her husband were living in a little log cabin. She remembers that he had asked her to go out and get something from outside of the cabin near a ravine. When she went out she saw an Indian standing beside a tree. Frightened she yelled for her husband to come out. She remembers her husband telling her not to move and then she saw him shoot the Indian in the stomach. It was a horrible dream but very real to her, for she felt the leaves crunching under her feet.

Although the conscious material was not overwhelming in terms of evidence, I decided to hypnotize her to see whether additional evidence might surface under hypnosis. Karen was fairly nervous but eventually calmed down sufficiently for me to be able to put her under. When I had reached 165 years prior to her birth she reported seeing a little boy with red hair but did not know who he was. At minus 200 however she described a village and someone named Molly. Molly was a four-year-old girl she knew then, she explained in the hypnotic state. I took Karen back to age eighteen, for Molly that is, and now there was also a boy named John Bradbury. The scene according to the hypnotized subject was England in the seventeen-hundreds and the location is called Abanel. Karen now became someone else, even to her facial expressions. Under questioning she disclosed that her name was Barbara and that her father was dead and that her mother was named Margaret. She was fifteen when I "found" her, but I quickly advanced Barbara to age twenty-five and discovered that she had had several children in the meantime, being now married to the aforesaid John Bradbury. At age forty, Barbara was still alive but "very tired," a grandmother now. Eventually she "just lays down and dies."

"After she dies what happens to her?" I inquired of the hypnotized subject.

"She just watches things and everybody."

"Where does she go?"

"Into the air."

"Does she meet anyone there whom she knows?"

"Papa."

"How long does she stay up there?"

"Until somebody needs her."

"Does Barbara get born again?"

11

"She just keeps looking around from there, looking at things."

"What is she looking for?"

"Probably John and her children."

I suggested that the subject follow Barbara forward in time until she reached another incarnation. "Where is Barbara now?"

"She's me, her name is Karen Lamb but they call her Kay."

"Does she know she's Barbara?"

"She could if she wanted to."

"Was there anything Barbara didn't finish that Kay could finish?"

"No, but she just shouldn't be unhappy. She's unhappy not knowing if she'll ever see her kids again."

I then changed my line of questioning, asking the subject to describe Barbara more closely.

"She has pretty hair in curls, green eyes and they sparkle when she smiles. Some women don't like her because of John Bradbury, he was Molly's boyfriend originally and he married Barbara. Molly married somebody else." Shortly afterwards I brought Karen out of her hypnotic state. On awakening she remembered absolutely nothing of what she had said while hypnotized. "I don't remember any Molly" she said firmly.

Juanita Thomson is a housewife in California. When she was about ten years old she had a vivid dream which she never forgot. In this dream she saw a street in a small town. So vivid was the dream that she was easily able to draw a picture of the vision. The road curved to the right and then led into town. There were hills on both sides, and in the center of the town there was a corner with a drugstore on it. In the dream, Mrs. Thomson had no idea why she was in that particular town, on that particular street. It reoccurred very vividly between ages 16 and 17. In June 1961, when she was eighteen years old, she was married. A few months afterwards her husband and she drove from Springfield, Missouri, to southern New Jersey. They took the northern route (route 66) that lead through parts of Ohio. When they neared the town of Zanesville, Mrs. Thomson seemed to feel that she had been there before; the road fit her dream experience. She did not make a point of it and they did not stop. But as they drove through town, she was suddenly thinking, "There are a lot more houses now." Since this was a unique experience, Mrs. Thomson wondered what it meant. "I have no idea what this is all about since I have not been east of Missouri except as an infant when my father was stationed in South Carolina."

Mr. K.S. is in his middle forties, well educated, married, an investment broker by profession and in his own words "steady and realistic." Here is his report, dated November 19, 1972.

"It was on April 9, 1971. I was at a Broadway play with my wife and there were about 500 or 600 people in the audience. We were seated in the eighth row center of the orchestra. It was 9:30 p.m., towards the end of the play and the footlights were soft. The leading lady had a minute or so of no dialogue and was seated facing the audience, twenty-eight or thirty feet from me. I had never seen her in person before and felt no more than a detached admiration for her, because I had seen her many times in a television series. Abruptly, she was staring at me. Thinking she was merely fixating, and trying to be gentlemanly, I closed my eyes momentarily. Her stare was still there when I opened them. That stare lasted not less than 30 seconds. But what had happened to me? While still aware of my body, I could swear that my head had become a separate entity converted into a radio receiver turned on and waiting for a message. Then, after a few seconds, it commenced to receive pulsation regularly at one per second, towards the end sounding like waves breaking on a distant shore. What happened to her? Her eyes, closed enough that the pupils and irises could be dis-

13

tinguished, and eventually from strain began to crinkle, as dried autumn leaves under a flame. Her face turned livid white. When her first dialogue came, she botched the words. Twenty minutes later, when the troupe took it's bows, she avoided any glance in my direction."

Although the observer would not divulge the name of this well-known actress, he promised to try and make contact with her to see whether she had experienced anything out of the ordinary at the same time as he had. He wondered whether his experience had anything to do with reincarnation. I assured him that similar "displacements" occur from time to time and may be indicative of reincarnation memories when someone who might have been a very close friend or an emotional attachment in a previous life, suddenly comes into view. One is unable to place the person correctly and tries very hard to do so.

The curious thing about these short flashes from another existence is that they occur, not only to people who may have an understanding of such previous situations, but frequently also to people to whom such earlier existences would be totally alien. When the information from a possible previous existence contains cultural, social or historical information not available to the person in the present, the evidential value of the observation is of course that much greater. Naturally, there are just as many cases where an individual experiences a reincarnation flash from a lifetime in similar surroundings to his present ones.

A good case in point, where great contrasts are obvious, is the case of Helen J. of Philadelphia, Pennsylvania. She has had a recurrent dream which was neither very long nor mysterious except that it involved her being in a place unknown to her in her present existence. "The place is a big house with a large number of rooms. There is a part of it which I keep locked up and do not use. Although I live in this place, there seems to be some anxiety, unhappiness, and even fear. In each dream it is exactly the same place, the same feeling. I have never lived in such a place and could never afford the furniture, such expensive furniture as it had. I am not interested in finding out whether I was great in another life. I would like to know what the dream means. I am a Negro of modest means and I consider myself intelligent, with some education."

Joseph K. of Southern California is in a parallel predicament. For eighteen years he has studied various aspects of metaphysics. His only regret is that these studies have Protestant overtones, while he's continually drawn to priests, nuns, cathedrals, and Catholic rituals. He even shows a penchant for this in his art. His best painting, *Port of Heavenly Revelation,* hangs in the chapel entrance of St. John's hospital in Santa Monica, California. He feels fulfilled by this, for he has always sensed that he owed something to the church. A medium friend assured him that he was a priest in his last existence. Mr. K. also writes music and poems, the latter strongly Catholic in tone and contents. The problem is, Mr. K. is Jewish.

Mrs. Helen Frank of Macon, Georgia, is a housewife. Her husband is a well-to-do-businessman, she has two grown sons and in her spare time she is the literary editor of *The Macon News.* She has always been interested in ESP, because she found that she possesses this power herself. On a number of occasions she would know events happening at a distance, and she has a very close telepathic relationship with both her children. But the experience that shook her up most happened in the summer of 1966 when she and her husband were in Europe, traveling through Italy. They were leaving the Trevi Fountain in Rome during a light rain, crossing a narrow street and hastening towards their waiting bus. Her husband was pulling her along, holding her by the hand so she wouldn't slip on the wet sidewalk. Suddenly she happened to gaze fleetingly at one of several small enclosed gardens. Peeking through one of the wrought-iron doors, she saw a place which she instantly knew she knew well though she had never seen it before. "I felt as though I were home. I knew that if I cast my eyes around to the right I would see a statue of a mother and child. If I looked to the left there would be an old tree with a bench around it. I did, and *they were there just as I knew they would be."*

But her husband was hurrying her back to the bus, so she could not stop and go in, though she wanted to very much. As he pulled her away, she recognized even the doorway of the house. Unfortunately they could not go back, because they left early the following morning. When she explained her startling experience to a friend the friend kiddingly called her "another Bridey Murphy." Until then Helen Frank had never heard of Bridey Murphy, but eventually she caught up with the book and understood the reference. That was all she could consciously remember. Nothing like it ever occurred to her again nor had anything like it happened to her before the incident in Rome. Under the circumstances, I suggested regression through hypnosis, and on my next visit to Atlanta, Georgia, we met for that purpose. That was on November 8, 1968, and after some initial conversation we went over the matter of the courtyard in Rome once again.

"All the houses were enclosed with high fences," she explained, "you could see through a gate into the yard and I was glancing at them as we went by. Suddenly I recognized the lintel over the door, that is the top part. I glanced at it and it looked very familiar, so I stopped and although my husband was pulling me and said, 'come on,' I said, 'wait just a minute,' and I stopped completely at the gateway and looked in and I recognized the whole yard. I didn't look at the house; somehow or other it didn't occur to me to look at the house, but the doorway in the yard I recognized immediately. I knew I had

16

been there. I knew that there would be the statue and over to the left an old tree with a bench of some sort around it and *I knew that I used to sit on it.* I looked for it and there it was."

"Did you see yourself in the picture?" I asked.

"I guess so," she replied, "but it was that courtyard that attracted me most strongly."

I proceeded to hypnotize her, with very poor results. For one reason or another, Mrs. Frank just wouldn't go under. After a while, I gave up and she returned to Macon.

I had instructed her to go over her entire past very calmly and as accurately as possible, and to report to me if she found anything unusual in her memories. On November 13, 1968, I heard from her again.

"I didn't tell you about something which I have always felt very strongly," she wrote, explaining that this had happened long before the incident in Italy. During the depression years, 1929 to 1935, her family was in financial difficulty. Everyone was very worried and talked constantly about being poor, but Helen just sat back and viewed the whole thing as if from a distant place. At the time, she was just sixteen years old but very mature for her age. She was told she couldn't have a new evening gown when she needed one and she saw her mother go to work for the first time. "But I went smoothly on my way, with the feeling that all of this was not happening to *me*, that I had always been very very wealthy and needed nothing *now*, that in the long ago I had had so much, that now it was rather fun not to have anything. Even my parents thought it strange that I never complained as the other kids did about doing without. It was like 'pretending to be poor' for me. I distinctly remember a time when there was no worry about money, that I had a vast amount of everything in the world." Helen Frank wonders whether her affluence had anything to do with the sudden memories of that little courtyard in Rome, Italy.

17

About three years ago I met Philip Kleinberg of Los Angeles. He is a teacher with some fifteen years of experience, has taught in elementary schools and in high schools as well, and is a part-time instructor at Los Angeles College. He holds a BA and MA degree from California State College. At present, Dr. Kleinberg is the Dean of the Southern California Institute of Graduate Studies as well. Dr. Kleinberg is a family man, widely read and not given to fantasizing. Nevertheless he has some experiences in the ESP field which he felt were worthy of my investigation. The incidents which Dr. Kleinberg felt might be indicative of reincarnation memories began in the spring of 1966. Leafing through a copy of the April 19, 1966, issue of *Look* magazine, he happened upon an article on Ireland, including some beautiful color photographs. As he turned the pages he suddenly stopped and, as he describes it, "became rooted to my seat as I gazed at one particular photograph on page 65. I felt not only déjà vu, that I had been there before, but also a deep longing to return to this lovely place and that something seemed to be drawing or pulling me right into the photograph itself. My reaction lasted about 30 seconds." When he recovered his balance, Dr. Kleinberg asked himself how a man of his background, American-born and of the Jewish faith, could be so emotionally responsive to an Irish scene. The photograph which had unsettled him was a picture of a cottage that had yellow-green farmland in the background. It is that part of the picture which so affected him. In the foreground was Dunbrody Abbey, built in 1182. The Abbey, or rather what is left of it, stands in County Wexford, Ireland. Although Dr. Kleinberg has had a number of psychic experiences, including trances, they do not bear directly upon any potential reincarnation memories. There is, however, a very interesting incident which seems to have a connection with his previous Irish flashback.

18

The Ulster incident took place December 23, 1969, and Dr. Kleinberg, with the sense of the orderly inherent in the teacher, recalls it was a Tuesday, between dawn and 8 a.m. While visiting relatives, he was staying at a motel in Fresno, California.

"I dreamt I saw the silhouette of a very tall man crossing a narrow, cobblestone street," Kleinberg explained to me when we met at the Continental Hotel in Hollywood. "The buildings, not too clear, were centuries old. There were no features that I could make out on the tall man, he was just a figure in black with a very long, loose coat or cloak and he wore a nineteenth-century black top hat. He seemed to glide swiftly across the cobblestone street in staccato fashion, moving from the foreground to the background of my dream. He never moved back and his movements were constantly repeated in moving *forward*. No one else was around. I felt that I was not in this scene but an observer looking in. The figure's movements became rapid. I found myself with an overwhelming feeling of panic, terror, and horror, and for no apparent reason.

"I then heard myself frantically shouting in cadence with the apparitions's movements: *'The Ulster is coming!'* I shouted this sentence aloud repeatedly and as fast as the figure moved, and the shouting volume also increased consistently.

"It was 8 a.m. when I awakened."

Five minutes later he related the "dream" to his wife, Irene, asking what Ulster meant to her. She thought it was a long coat. Kleinberg himself had no idea of the meaning of the word, except that he had of course heard it. His curiosity aroused, he looked it up in the dictionary and found a reference not only to a coat but also to Ulster Province, Northern Ireland.

During the next few days, when the impression remained vivid to him, Kleinberg tried to puzzle it out. Then on December 28, 1969, five days afterwards, he happened to hear a news broadcast while driving, in which the newscaster referred to the then current political flareups in Belfast, Ulster. It brought back his dream impression. Another news item referring to continuing strife in Ulster which he happened to hear a month later gave Kleinberg the feeling that his psychic experience was merely refering to this situation in Ulster and thus was of a clairvoyant nature. Curiously, it never occurred to him to connect the two Irish experiences with each other, i.e. his déjà vu feeling on seeing a magazine picture and the dream.

And yet, they belong together, it seems to me.

What exactly did Dr. Kleinberg tune in on from the past, *his* past?

The man in the black coat may have been someone in authority, on the Irish side that is, organizing an uprising perhaps. The Irish revolutionaries of the nineteenth century generally wore dark clothes, in order to be less conspicuous, but also as a symbol of morning for Irish liberties taken away by the British. As for the sentence, shouted in panic, 'The Ulster is coming!', I think this might also refer to the sudden arrival of a British-led regiment, the Ulster Cuirassiers, in order to put down the uprising by the Irish people.

Perhaps, if Dr. Kleinberg has another "dream" of his Irish past, we can be more certain of this. Meanwhile it remains an interesting, though fragmentary experience pointing to another lifetime before the present one.

Of all the human relationships that seem to endure, the love relationship between men and women appears to be the most powerful. At any rate, the number of cases involving such relationships which has come to my attention is far greater than any other relationships in possible past lives.

Ruth Poland has had many kinds of jobs over the years; she is a natural artist even though she has had no formal training, and she has lived in the south as well as in California. Another characteristic of hers is a special liking for people with dark skins, such as Mexicans or Indians. Her inclination towards such people was unconscious and very subtle, but it was nevertheless expressed in many ways. At the time she was managing a nightclub at a motel in Phoenix, Arizona, a friend arranged for a blind date for her. While her friend's back was turned, a man stepped into the busy nightclub; she instantly recognized him, went to him and embraced him and he her as if they had been lifelong friends. Both of them said, simultaneously, "It is so good to see you *again*," although neither had met the other before. Their relationship was instantaneous and very close. He was part Indian. When he died rather suddenly, Ruth felt as if she had lost everything. Sometime after her friend's death, she moved to Texas in order to forget him. It was about a year later, when she came home from work, rather tired; she kicked off her shoes and lay down across the bed to go through the day's mail. As she looked up at the ceiling she noticed that it was suddenly transformed into a kind of a movie screen. Before her eyes she saw a story unfold. She knew that the location was Canada and she could see herself kneeling by a stream. "The water was as clear as glass and I could see my reflection in it, even though there was a waterfall nearby and I could feel the fine misty spray from it on my face. Behind me was the forest with large trees. I felt anxious but happy for I was to meet someone there, and as I looked into the water another face appeared from behind me. I could see myself smiling and feel my heart fairly swell with happiness. He took my hand and lifted me to my feet, and though I couldn't see his face clearly, I knew he was an Indian. We were both dressed in tan buckskin, his chest was bare and he had a band around his wrist and a white feather at the back of his head. The only words we spoke were our names as we met; he said, 'Ruda,' I said 'Ra-u,' as he led me into the forest. There seemed to be an urgency to be away from there before we were discovered. For some reason or

21

another, someone was trying to keep us apart and we were running away together."

Before Miss Poland could think over what she had just seen in her vision, another scene appeared to her. This time she could not see herself in it but felt as if it happened inside of her. She could feel herself standing in the shade of a balcony. "I could feel the heat rising up from the desert in front of me. The sand was yellow turning to red in the distance and I was looking at a pyramid. I knew inside it was my father and I was unhappy and I could hear myself say, 'Oh father, please don't let them send me away, I'm so afraid I shall never see my beautiful Egypt again.' " The next moment the vision was gone, but her face was wet with tears. She was not asleep when this happened, only normally tired. It was a beautiful spring day and she could not have been "overheated." Moreover, Miss Poland had not read any stories or seen any movies or television shows pertaining to Egypt.

But her visions kept plaguing her and she wondered if she could recall them at will. Whenever she came home she would try to recreate the circumstances during which the visions had last appeared to her, lying on her bed and looking up at the ceiling and waiting. Nothing happened for a month. Then, just as suddenly and unexpectedly as before, she knew she was somewhere else. "I could hear two men talking at first and I thought it was someone in the next apartment or the one above me, as it seemed the voices were above me and getting louder all the time, but then I realized I was not in my apartment but in a garage and of all places under the mechanic's bench. I was hiding there but don't know why. Suddenly I panicked as 'they' got too close and I yelled out, 'don't step on me.' The last thing I remember were the shocked expressions on two men's faces. Later my landlady dropped by and said she wondered about the voices she had heard from my apartment and thought I had had company."

But time is a healer and Ruth met another man to whom she felt herself strongly attached. She and her gentleman friend became lovers and their feelings were both mutual and very deep. One day she saw him standing in the bathroom, shaving; his face was in darkness. All she could see were his trousers and his chest and arms were bare. She heard herself say to him, "Ra-u." Her friend was not surprised, since his name was Raul. Though her friend is not a free man, he feels very deeply for Ruth. She wonders whether Ra-u and Raul are one and the same person, and whether she knew him in ancient America.

There are cases which may be due to reincarnation memories or perhaps only communications from restless spirit personalities, using a living person to express themselves. By impressing the living "partner," telling their stories, they relive themselves of their pent-up emotional problems and thus find a degree of release in the process. Some of these cases are difficult to decide, because the criteria are equally hard to define. By and large, I feel that previous ESP incidents, that is the realization of reincarnation memories indicate the possibility of spirit communication. The total absence of any other psychic experiences, either before the reincarnation memory is realized or after, I take for strong proof that genuine reincarnation memories are being dealt with.

Verda Sanders is in the fish-hatchery business in California. For many years she has been puzzled by an odd experience which to her could not be explained on rational grounds. "Several times I seemed to be awakened by some woman calling, 'Come!'" she explained. "I was not asleep when I actually *saw* her, a figure of a woman, running, but pausing and half turning back to call to me and pointing in the direction she had been running. This was at the Amelia Earhart Hotel at a base in Germany. She always appeared to me wearing a long dress, of about the middle eighteen-hundreds, and she had a slim figure and was beautiful, with long yellow hair. She was

23

young, perhaps in her twenties to early thirties, and she ran lightly; I don't know whether I saw her bare feet but the way she was running left the impression in my mind that she might have been barefoot. Her dress was simple and of rather thin material, but she seemed to be solid enough and complete from head to foot."

Miss Sanders saw the apparition daily for a week, then she had to leave for London. This happened in the summer of 1966. Each time the girl appeared to Miss Sanders, she spoke, urging her to follow. "She would say, 'Come, come here!' two or three times and then just disappear. I never spoke to her as I was always trying to figure out just what she meant and then she didn't stay long either."

Several days after Miss Sanders arrived in London, she realized, almost with disappointment, that her lady had not come along with her. One morning, however, she appeared to her again; this time she seemed quite impatient and almost angry with her and again demanded that Miss Sanders come with her, adding the word "now" to her command. Miss Sanders saw her once more, just after she came back to Germany. This time the scene was different, however. "It was as if I had just approached, uphill and around a bend, a lovely little narrow dead-end canyon with trees, a creek and a small lake with a small tree-covered island near it. I saw her sitting on a little knoll and I stopped. She was wearing a very pensive and almost sad expression and looking either at the lake or the small island. I had the feeling she had been waiting for me but she didn't look at me or speak to me; yet I knew she knew that I was there. At first I felt that I had "come" too late; but I don't think that was the reason she seemed rather sad and lonely. Although she appeared to be very solid and real, her hair and dress were shimmering in the light like moonlight." Miss Sanders isn't quite sure how the vision ended, whether she went back to sleep and dreamed the final portion or whether she received it telepathically, but it seemed to her that the woman's name was Emaline or Emaleen. She also felt that someone lay buried on that small island. On recollection, Miss Sanders realized it was never necessary for her to speak to the apparition, as though she knew what she was thinking. Objectively, Miss Sanders does not know anyone looking like the apparition but the dream canyon represents the ideal spot she would like to find in this life. Naturally, Miss Sanders began to wonder whether her imagination had played her tricks; it never occurred to her that it might be the other way around and that her longing for just such a canyon and little island was inspired by an actual experience there in another lifetime.

There have been some isolated incidents of psychic ability in Miss Sanders' life, both before and after the visions of the strange lady. Shortly after writing to me about her experiences, she returned to the United States on a disability retirement and moved to Southern California. She hasn't seen the lovely lady and her little island since.

Short scenes, sudden flashes of a previous existence, sudden recognition of places or people one has not consciously encountered before are difficult to check and nearly always escape objective verification simply because the material is usually too limited. There are, however, many instances of longer scenes or memories along the same lines, where objective verification is possible and I shall deal with them in the next chapter. Drawing conclusions from longer stories or experiences, I am convinced that the shorter experiences are no less valid, no less true, even if they are more difficult to prove than are the extended experiences.

Chapter 2
Specific Cases
of Identifiable Personalities
and Detailed Memories

Some reincarnation cases involve prolonged experiences, recurrent dreams with sufficient development within them to make for a detailed story. Other cases, such as those reported by me in *Born Again,* especially the one about Pat Wollenberg of Harvey, Illinois, and Ruth MacGuire, may have stretched over several weeks or even months and usually involve hypnotic regression to deepen the original material and find additional information. I have always felt that claims to have been somebody very famous in history are likely to be false or, at the very least, exaggerated or not capable of objective verification. One should not take such a statement as being 100 percent untrue either since there are cases involving historical personalities that may very well be authentic. The difficulty lies not so much in categorizing the reincarnation material as historically famous or historically unknown, as in the kind of evidence that would hold up when we are dealing with historically well-known individuals. Quite naturally, if the claimant refers to a celebrated personality, much if not all of the published material about that personality should be discounted and the fact that it was accessible taken into account. On the other hand, if the claimant comes up with personal material of the kind that is not found in ordinary books or the kind of sources available to the general public, but is later verified through research, possibly through unpublished documents or otherwise hidden materials, then we cannot deny the possibility that a famous personality has been reincarnated in our time, In my earlier work on reincarnation, I reported the case of Mrs. Catherine Warren-Browne of England and later of California, who had a detailed and very specific memory of life at the court of King Henry VIII. Because of the highly personal and private nature of the material coming to her, both in the dream state and under hypnotic regression, I came to the conclusion that Mrs. Warren-Browne was indeed the reincarnated Queen Catherine Paar.

As the result of appearing on Boston television, co-hosting the morning program, I received a number of reports concerning psychic phenomena. Among the reports there was one from a lady of "proper Bostonian background," the wife of a prominent executive, mother of two children and very much concerned with the details of daily living in a stately house in one of the suburbs of Boston. I was so impressed with the sincerity and apparent objectivity of Mrs. Charlotte Tuton's report, that I telephoned her and asked her to come and see me next time I was in Boston again.

The meeting took place in early March 1972, and we were able to go over the entire experience in greater detail than on the telephone.

Mrs. Tuton graduated from Wellesley College in 1958. Primarily scholastically oriented, she happened to read one of Ruth Montgomery's books and immediately opened a correspondence with her concerning some occult experiences she had had during her life. At that point also Mrs. Tuton became interested in finding out about any possible previous lives. Since age eleven she had had a strong attachment to the person of

Anne Boleyn, the unfortunate wife of Henry VIII of England who paid with her life for an alleged indiscretion. "Many features of my own life and circumstances lead me to believe that either I was her, or was very closely associated with her," Mrs. Tuton explained. "It didn't occur to me to put all of these varied clues together until rather recently, but I have lived with them all my life."

Somehow, at the tender age of eleven, she happened on a book called *Brief Gaudy Hour* by Margaret Campbell. The book dealt with the life of Anne Boleyn and upset her greatly, to an extent that nothing ever affected her again in her later years, even though she has read scores upon scores of other books, including historical novels. In addition, all her life she had had an almost automatic psychological reaction of terror at the thought of knives or any sharp metallic objects. No other weapon seemed to frighten her in the least but the very thought of mentioning blades of any kind produced an attack of goose bumps and shivers in her. Frequently she experienced the severe sensation of the cutting of a major nerve or nerves in the back of her neck. This physical feeling became so intense that she consulted a neurosurgeon at the Lahey Clinic. No known physiological cause for the sensation could be found. Nevertheless, it continued to appear from time to time. Mrs. Tuton also makes something out of the fact that her given names were Charlotte and Anne. From her earliest recollections she had always told her mother that Charlotte was the wrong name for her that she should have been called only Anne. She had been named Charlotte after her mother, but her mother did not follow thr r ·gh with her own second name instead took Anne from an obscure relative.

As the years went on, Mrs. Tuton had a rather strong feeling that she had lost a way of life in high places, among people whose decisions affected the course of history at every turn. At the same time, there was an accompanying sense of having been wrongly accused of some act that she did not commit. "None of these feelings can be explained in any way by my present lifetime," she explained. Perhaps it is only a "coincidence" if there be such a thing, that Anne Boleyn died in 1536 while Mrs. Tuton was born in 1936, exactly four hundred years later.

Less likely to be coincidental was an incident in May 1965 when Mrs. Tuton was having lunch with her husband in a Paris restaurant. A stranger kept staring at her from across the room. Finally he got up, approached her table and, asking her forgiveness, wondered if he could join them for a few moments. It turned out that he was an English parapsychologist attending a convention dealing with his subject. He informed Mrs. Tuton that she had significant talent in this field and urged her to pursue it. "Over the years, several people have stopped me on the street, approached me in supermarkets, and once again, very memorably, in a Boston restaurant, to ask, "Who *are* you?" Mrs. Tuton reported. "And knowing that they are not asking my name as such, I must ask, with them *who?*"

I began to regress Mrs. Tuton hypnotically but to my chagrin, and, I am sure to hers, we were unable to get her under. After half an hour we gave up. Perhaps being so close to a possible solution of the enigma was too much for Mrs. Tuton: the excitement may have been the very thing that kept her from letting go. *Was* she Anne Boleyn? Being affected by the fate of the unlucky queen and any material pertaining to it would not necessarily indicate that she was; it is more likely that she may have been someone very close to the queen, perhaps a noble lady attending upon her.

In November 1972 I received a strange letter from a man in Montreal. Joe Levi, 37 years old, consultant and owner of a large firm in the field of business interiors explained that he had been interested in the question of life after death since he was fifteen and had come across a case of reincarnation which he wished to discuss with me. It involved his own brother, Ike. The material had been discovered accidentally when Ike underwent hypnotic regression in Montreal. Mr. Levi wondered whether I might be interested in seeing the material, and came to discuss the case with me in New York. With the two young men was a friend and advisor, a Mr. Ozy Paulik, also from Montreal.

The whole thing started when Mr. Levi himself wanted to be hypnotized and had gone to a professional hypnotist by the name of Henry Spivak. Unfortunately, Mr. Levi was unable to be hypnotized and suggested that the hypnotist try to work with his brother instead. It turned out that the brother was an excellent subject. The brother, Ike Banoun, having been born in Cairo, Egypt, never had had any conscious memories of previous lives. He has done no reading on the subject of reincarnation, never met anyone whom he thought he had known before, or in any way shown an interest in the occult. Prior to joining his brother in Montreal, he had lived in New York for eleven years where he had received his education. The hypnotist did not believe in reincarnation. According to the hypnotist, the human mind was able to fabricate all sorts of fantasies to please the hypnotist, and the material had to be viewed in that light. Just the same, Mr. Banoun subjected himself to the hypnotic regression treatment. During the first four visits, the hypnotist did not go beyond the threshhold of birth but stopped at the teen-age level. Only after that did actual regression into a possible previous existence begin. At age eleven the subject reverted to French. This was only natural since he had spoken that language in his earlier years; as the hypnotist spoke only English, this presented a problem, but he continued to take the subject back beyond birth. For a long time there was no answer. Everything was in French now and Mr. Levi acted as interpreter. The hypnotist would suggest, "You are in the body of a previous person," and would ask the subject to tell them who he was.

"It took a while," Mr. Levi explained, "but then somebody speaking through Ike said, 'What the hell are you talking about?' This was in English, mind you, in reply to a French question."

At that point, apparently, another personality took over Ike. "He said he was a person by the name of Larry Maldi, and that he was working for the mob. He was a runner for the mob," Mr. Levi explained. Larry Maldi gave explicit details about his life in New York and New Jersey, especially about Queens and the Bronx. He claimed that he had been an orphan, and that his father died when he was seven years old. He mentioned working for the Italian underground as many mobsters did during the war. Interestingly, he spoke in Italian. Mr. Levi was able to confirm this since he speaks Italian while his brother does not. The reincarnated mobster explained that he had been shot on February 27, 1942, on Fifth Avenue, from a speeding car.

"Was he aware that he was dead?" I asked. "Yes," Mr. Levi replied, "he felt his death; he felt that he was dying and saw a little girl taking him by the hand and leading him away." The experimenters then asked for the mobster's father and, the father, John Maldi, also spoke through the entranced Ike.

The hypnotist remained skeptical about the surprising material, confirming only that the subject was definitely in trance, that is, deeply under hypnosis. Ike later listened to the tapes of his sessions with the hypnotist. He cannot remember anything from the time that he was under hypnosis, and is just as skeptical about the whole thing as the hypnotist, but frankly interested. He doesn't care whether or not he was Larry Maldi, New York mobster, but is satisfied to be Ike Banoun in this life.

In discussing the recent publication of *Sigmund Freud and Lou Andreas-Salomé Letters* edited by Ernst Pfeiffer, Paul A.

Robertson, in a book review in *The New York Times,* March 11, 1973, states, "Lou Andreas-Salomé was a woman famous for the men she knew. The formidable roster of her acquaintances included most of the Central European luminaries of her generation (she was born in 1861) among them Arthur Schnitzler, Ferdinand Toennies, Gerhart Hauptmann, Frank Wedekind, and Martin Buber. The three most notable men in her life, however, were Friedrich Nietzsche, who reputedly proposed to her, Rainer Maria Rilke, who became her lover, and Sigmund Freud, to whose teaching she attached herself from 1911 to her death in 1937."

Two years before this book appeared in print, I was handed a brief note by my good friend Sara Cunningham, a teacher of witchcraft and the occult in Pasadena, California. It was from a young woman who wanted to get in touch with me, desperately as it were, to find out about her reincarnation memories. Helen, who has since married and presumably forgotten all about her previous problems, came to see me at the Hollywood Continental Hotel shortly afterwards. A slim, attractive young girl, she seemed nevertheless unusually nervous. "I was baptized and raised a Catholic," she explained, "and until last August had no belief in anything occult, in fact went through periods of atheism and agnostism. In college I studied comparative religion and philosophy but came out without conclusions."

"What is the problem, or rather what is the proof you have of having been someone specific before?" I asked, since she had mentioned reincarnation memories. Helen looked me straight in the face and said, "I'm the daughter of an American admiral. Throughout my life I have been keenly interested in writing and last year I found myself working on a novel for a New York publisher. It was actually a rewrite of a book I had written when I was seventeen years old and is the love story of a young girl who falls in love with an older man, a philosopher-politician; it is set in Eastern Europe, on the Russian border. The culmination of their affair takes place in a mountain retreat. While I was writing this book, I wanted at one point to quote something from Nietzsche. I had never studied him because I disliked his view of the world, but in this chapter my heroine is in the garden of an Albanian philosopher, trimming vines off his African baobab tree. They mention Nietzsche in their conversation and I figured it would be relevant. I went to a philosophical compendium belonging to my fiance, flipped it open to the section on Nietzche, and the very first paragraph that hit my eye was Nietzsche's discussion of the tree of man overrun and destroyed by the vines of love. It was this first, baffling coincidence, that began so much."

"Go on," I said, waiting patiently for something evidential.

"Throughout my life, there have been coincidences with the life of Lou Andreas-Salomé, the student-lover of Friedrich Nietzsche. She was born in 1861 in St. Petersburg, and met him when she was just twenty-one. She was the daughter of a Russian general, an intellectual, and claimed that she was the only woman Nietzsche ever asked to marry him. He was famous for his hatred of women. The love story is unclear, despite a series of letters. The leading theory is that she jilted him for another man; he suffered one of his many breakdowns during that period. She is considered to have contributed a great deal to the bitterness which helped him create his Anti-Christ and Dionysian view of mankind as two races of masters and slaves. After Nietzsche died, insane, Andreas-Salomé became a famous female intellectual. She wrote a series of novels and became a student of Freud. She became one of the first female psychoanalysts in Europe. She died in 1937 in Germany as Hitler was rising to power. When she died, she was trying to write a refutation of *The Anti-Christ.*

I had not even heard of Andreas-Salomé until last August but now I began to read. The first novel she wrote in 1886 was inspired by her first meeting with Nietzsche in the Swiss mountains at a mountain retreat called Sils-Maria. The heroine of that novel was named Jane. Please note that the heroine of my own novel, written long before I knew of this, was Jayne, and their mountain retreat was called Baia Mare."

I was impressed. If what Helen told me was factual, and I had no reason to doubt it at this point, this was more than coincidence. Such closeness of fictional names, without any overt possibility of one being derived from the other consciously, cannot be explained as mere "coincidence." But I wanted to hear more about Helen's alleged incursions from Lou Andreas-Salomé.

"When I was six years old," she continued her narrative, "my family was living in Seattle, Washington. At that time, I used to talk a great deal about 'the man on the Olympic mountain.' Mount Olympus, of course, barricades Seattle from the West. Much later, when writing my novel, I discovered Nietzsche's view that the masters of men live on a metaphorical Olympic mountain."

There were a number of events and "coincidences" linking Helen with the celebrated love and student of Nietzsche. For months, Helen would be plagued "by the observed idea of a llama just before falling asleep. The day after it first occurred to me, I was looking up the word in the dictionary and encountered a picture of the exact llama I had seen—an alpaca with dark fur. Later I read that Nietzsche's nickname for his sister was, 'the llama.' " On another occasion Helen used the image of Lewis Carroll's opium-smoking caterpillar in her writing; then she discovered that it was a requote of a description Nietzsche had written of the future of America, using the metaphor of the American Indian.

For many years, Helen had admired and considered herself in

love with a well-known writer-philosopher. He looked exactly like Nietzsche; his latest book had dealt with a discussion of the human will, but in it he had left the explanation to magic, claiming that life was a problem for the Magic Will. "Before Nietzsche died," Helen explained with a significant nod, "he said that if he were ever reincarnated, he would come back as 'a teller of bad jokes and a dabbler in magic'; my writer-philosopher friend also shows a comical vein in his work."

Despite their close relationship, Helen hesitated to acquaint her friend with the amazing parallels between their lives and those of Nietzsche and Lou Andreas-Salomé. She feared that he would be too cynical and realistic to believe it. But she kept a list of all her thoughts, feelings and ideas about him. Eventually, a year before she came to see me, she handed him this list. On it were thoughts he had expressed on paper without anyone else's knowledge, including a story that appeared in print two weeks *after* Helen gave him the information!

I hypnotized Helen, but found only the same basic material she had reported to me. Apparently, she was one of those rare cases where the reincarnation material is completely in the conscious mind and need not be ferreted out from the deeper layers of the unconscious. I heard from her again about a year later. Her fiance had become her husband and somehow the stabilization of her emotional life had helped blend the two personalities of the nineteenth-century woman and the twentieth-century girl into one fully resolved individual; what residues of frustration remained in her, Helen will undoubtedly be able to express through her writings.

Mrs. Audrey Holmes is in her late thirties, an Englishwoman married twelve years, with three children, and living, in her own words, "a quiet family life in a split-level suburban home" in Canada where she immigrated in 1960. Her educational background included two years at a Bible college and one year at midwifery in London; she graduated as a registered nurse at age twenty-one. In July 1967, seven years after she had arrived in Canada, she gradually became aware of some unseen entities around her. It gave her a sense of peace, "of being uplifted in my inner being." Two years after her arrival in Canada she moved to the little town of Ancaster in Ontario and has been there ever since. The peculiar experience lasted for about three months and Mrs. Holmes was wondering whether she was being prepared for something that was to follow. Various psychic experiences happened to her in those days, such as knowing what patient in the hospital she was working in would die soon. At various times she felt a Presence around her. All this was at variance with her training and background, of course, and she tried her best to dissuade herself from believing it. Nevertheless, all sorts of psychic experiences and visions kept coming to her.

Despite a long history of psychic experiences, going back into her childhood and student days, Mrs. Holmes was terribly shaken by a vivid dream she had in late June 1969. In the dream, she was aware of having lived in the same village of Ancaster during the early nineteenth century. Details of buildings and roads came to her and were remembered clearly the following morning. Her curiosity led her to the Ancaster Historic Society where she was able to ascertain that the descriptions she had received during the dream were indeed correct for the period involved. In particular, Mrs. Holmes had been impressed by two buildings. With the help of two books, *The History of St. John's Anglican Church* and *Wentworth Landmarks,* published in 1897 and dealing with historical buildings in Wentworth County in which Ancaster is located, she was able to identify them. One she found to have been Leeming Parsonage, erected in 1816, and the other the old tannery which she found sketched in *Wentworth Landmarks.* Prior to the dream, Mrs. Holmes had had absolutely no knowledge of Ancaster's past, nor had she had access to any information or illustrations concerning the buildings she saw in her dream. Mrs. Holmes discussed her experience with the members of The Ancaster Historical Society and also communicated the dream experience to Dr. Ian Stevenson, University of Virginia, Charlottesville, Virginia, whose field of study is reincarnation.

During the summer of 1969 she and her husband drove down to Buffalo. On their way back to Canada they passed by Niagara Lake. They stopped near Niagara-on-the-Lake, close to the shore. There were a few sailing boats and children on the beach and it was a very peaceful quiet scene. Suddenly it all seemed very familiar to Mrs. Holmes. She could have sworn that she and her husband had been there before, when in fact they had not. She laid down a few minutes to rest and suddenly she remembered.

"I saw myself in my mind's eye as a young woman, walking down the road with an older woman and a child, and I could almost feel the long gray dress clinging to my legs." This was about two months after the initial dream of a previous life in Ancaster. In discussing her experience at Niagara with the secretary of the Ancaster Historical Society, she learned that Ancaster's early settlers came from upper Canada via the Niagara River, and were called the United Empire Loyalists.

Returning to the exact location of a previous life is comparatively rare in the annals of reincarnation research. Perhaps, Audrey Holmes had not been able to complete her first experience in Ancaster and was therefore "sent" back to the same location to pick up where she had left off. Unfortunately, Mrs. Holmes has had no further flashes of that previous existence. Sometimes reincarnation memories end when they have been brought to the surface of the conscious mind. In realizing that one has lived before at some place or other, the need to externalize the buried information no longer exists and the sensation ceases.

38

Chapter 3
Children and Reincarnation

It is not uncommon for a young child to speak of places, situations, and people a child couldn't possibly have known. Those unfamiliar with the record of reincarnation research are quick to attribute all such unusual utterances to childish fantasies. But what is one to make of entire sentences, formed by a two- or three-year-old child, using words the child could not possibly have heard or absorbed even if they have been spoken in his immediate family? What is one to make of complicated, even sophisticated, descriptions of places from the historical past in households where history is not a household word. The number of cases where small children, even as little as one year old, speak in coherent and intelligent fashion of places and people they could not possibly know, apart from the fact that they could not possibly speak in such a fashion anyway, is impressive. Some of these cases have been called miracle children, or *Wunderkinder*. With very rare exceptions, however, they are not miracle children, but only children who happen to remember something from their earlier lives. Even those few who are genuine miracle children are very likely to be in that position, not due to some special talent within themselves, but because of what they have brought into this life from another one.

In the majority of cases that have come to my attention, the ability to recall seeming bits and pieces from an earlier lifetime gradually fade out towards the time when the child goes to school. In some cases the memory returns around ages seventeen or eighteen, and then usually with a vengeance and in greater detail. But at that point the rational capacity of the person as well as some educational background must be taken into account when evaluating the evidence. With a little child below the age of five such problems are of less impact. On the average, a child begins to speak in coherent sentences after age two, in many cases only when reaching age three. The ability to describe places and situations outside the immediate family does not usually begin until age four or five. Even if one takes a certain amount of fantasy into account, and many children refer to invisible friends as part of their development, there remains a hard core of evidential cases where all these explanations must be ruled out.

Closely related to reincarnation memories by children are the descriptive utterances concerning the in-between state, after one death and prior to a rebirth. The material on that in-between stage in which the soul is between assignments, so to speak, is not as plentiful as one would like it to be. Whatever evidential material is available, however, shows a remarkable amount of duplication, leading me to believe that the information comes from a single source, quite possibly the truth. In this respect one should also classify here material pertaining to the reception of a new baby in the family, when the experience occurs to the parent but deals with the expected child.

A good case of the latter is the already mentioned case of Diane Rogers of Chicago, Illinois. Miss Rogers contacted me because she wanted some sort of an explanation for her many ESP experiences and for some material that seemed to her to indicate reincarnation memories.

"What was the first thing that tipped you off that you had some sort of special gift?" I asked her. "The first thing I remember was a dream. I was twenty-two years old at the time and expecting a baby. In my dream I was also expecting a baby and the child was being born. It was a girl and I saw myself with the child in a restaurant; it was a vivid dream. At the time I was about seven months pregnant." "Did you have a baby girl afterwards?" "Yes, and after the child was born she looked exactly as I had seen her in my dream. In the dream she looked approximately four months old. She wore a yellow dress with white lace and puffed sleeves and in the dream I saw ourselves in a restaurant that I didn't know at the time. When the baby was four months old, we did find ourselves in such a restaurant in Lansing, Illinois, and the child was wearing the identical clothes I had seen her wear in the dream."

If this had been merely a precognitive dream concerning a little girl it would not be a matter for us to discuss here in a book dealing with reincarnation. But the fact that Mrs. Rogers saw her little baby girl while she was still carrying her makes this a case of some interest for us: quite clearly, some superior force or law had already determined what the baby would look like and what its future attachments would be. Mrs. Rogers was merely being given an advance view of what she could expect.

Patricia Ladd of Kentucky is a housewife in her late thirties, mother of three children, and used to having ESP experiences from childhood on. She has worked at various odd jobs, from waiting on tables to decorating to an electrical assembly line. She and her family live in a hundred-year-old house in suburban Kentucky. The house is haunted by the spirit of an earnest, slender, dark-eyed young woman, who has appeared to Mrs.

Ladd carrying an infant in her arms. Mrs. Ladd has heard footsteps and all sorts of human noises in the house. She realizes she's psychic and the ghosts don't really bother her very much. Her children are aware of the phenomena, too.

One night, when everyone was fast asleep, except her son, little Eddie, she said, playfully, "Eddie, where did you come from?" Earnestly the little boy replied, "From heaven." When his mother looked at him questioningly, he added, "I mean that before I was born I was a ghost like you talk about." "Have you ever been on earth before?" asked the mother. The little boy nodded, "Yes, I was waiting around, waiting to be born." Mrs. Ladd was nonplussed. "Where will you go when you die, Eddie?" she said. "Back to God and wait to be born again." At the time of this conversation Eddie was twelve years old.

Darlene Jones is a housewife in Southern California. Her husband is part owner of a motorcycle and automobile agency, and they have one son and twin girls, the latter only seventeen months old at the time Mrs. Jones communicated with me in the fall of 1970. Mrs. Jones has no artistic training whatsoever but likes to draw and paint whenever she feels like it, and during the last few years has felt more and more compelled to express herself in this manner. But she considered herself strictly an amateur and has no artistic ambitions whatsoever. In 1968 she completed a large painting, originally meant to be a painting of flowers, three blooms in three stages; opening bud, half open, and full bloom, the symbolic lotus. Mrs. Jones had toyed with the idea of superimposing a small woman's figure in the center, awakening and rising like an oriental dancer. "This figure was to be added over the flowers when the painting was finished and I had chosen a title. It was to be called 'The Unfolding of Self.' How appropriate it was I had no idea," Mrs. Jones explained.

"It was in the spring of 1968. I was working with only two

colors, yellow and a rusty brown. I am such an amateur painter that I just paint and I'm not sure of the technical ways of colors. It had been in the beginning stages for months but I had only parts of two of the flowers and was working on the third. On this particular day I had been painting for a while and had stopped to rest. I left the room and later when I returned, I was startled to see the upper part of the woman's face, eyes, and nose in the painting. Even though I had considered maybe adding a dancer later, this definitely was not what I had had in mind. I was startled because I truly had only been painting flowers. It seemed to be an accident and so I thought I would complete the face, put in the mouth and chin. Taking up the paint brush, I tried to apply paint in this area. *I couldn't.* Every time I approached this part of the canvas with a brush it was as though I encountered a mound, a round object that I could not get past. It had a definite feeling of a ball, a round object."

This happened in the first week of June, 1968. Mrs. Jones continued to paint her flowers around this mound which would not let her pass by. "By this time it had very obviously become the round head of a fair-haired baby. Yet at no time had I painted anything except flowers," Mrs. Jones explained. "Then the 'flowers' were completed on June 25 or 26, 1968, and I placed the finished painting, now showing a face and a baby on the fireplace mantle." As yet Mrs. Jones had no idea what was going on with her painting. One of the first visitors to see this painting completed was her brother, Dennis Shunn. He entered the room, looked at the painting, and remarked, "You have two babies," and pointed at the spot in the painting where he saw two little babies, one behind the other. "I looked and there in the painting I had painted I saw what I had not seen before: there were and are two babies, one fair and husky, one dark and petite. They were enough different in size that we thought that one might be a boy and the other a girl, but time and circum-

43

stances have proved differently. A psychic friend who saw the painting commented that the "little one was the oldest. Actually, she was, by four minutes."

The realization that the faces of two babies had somehow appeared in her painting as if by themselves, and the recognition of this strange development by others happened during the last week of June 1968. Nine months later on March 27, 1969, Mrs. Jones gave birth to twin girls. The older one turned out to be petite and dark, the younger one fair and husky, exactly as in the painting. "Had they announced their coming in the painting that had been completed the very week, possibly the very day, of their *conception?*" Mrs. Jones asked herself. To her that was the only answer to the painting of "flowers" which turned out to have the images of children not yet born.

Early in her pregnancy she had told her doctor that she would bear twins. He assured her that she was mistaken. Later, he was a very surprised doctor, but Mrs. Jones did not mention the painting to him. During the period in which she was pregnant, Mrs. Jones had a number of visitors come to her house and look at the painting. Spontaneously, people remarked about two forms between the figure of the woman and the two babies. A psychic friend by the name of Stan Reid saw these additional figures in July of 1968 and remarked that he thought that they were spirits waiting to come into this world. At that time Mrs. Jones was not yet aware of her pregnancy. Others who saw the two figures hovering near the heads of the babies at a time when Mrs. Jones was not yet aware of her pregnancy include her secretary and friend, Carole Krugger, her sister-in-law Ellen Shunn, and her brother Dennis Shunn.

"There are other things in this painting," Mrs. Jones added, "it gives me a good feeling and is totally unlike anything I have ever done. As an added touch there are tiny horns on the fair child and sketchy but definitely visible wings on the other. The wings were at a place where I had started to place a petal but changed my mind. *Still, I was only painting flowers.* The peculiar part is that these are true insights into the babies; one is a dominant, aggressive, mischievous child (horns), and the other is so sweet and giving like an angel (wings). Already at seventeen months she uses 'thank you' about twenty times a day without being prompted."

Mrs. Jones let me have a set of photographs of the remarkable painting, which would be a fine work of art regardless of the reincarnation connotations. The twins standing before the painting, created while they were still in limbo, are exactly as they are being depicted in the painting. Even the facial expressions are the same.

Prior to her first visit to the doctor and prior to her knowledge of her pregnancy, Mrs. Jones had a prophetic dream. In this dream vision she seemed worried that she did not have a picture of the father of her children. She confided this worry to her closest friend, Carole, and the latter said that she should not worry about a picture of him because she had two *in the camera.* Immediately after having this dream, she related it to her friend, Carole Krugger, and thus has a witness to it. In retrospect, it is clear to Mrs. Jones that the dream referred to the two "images" of her husband within herself, she herself being the camera. It indicates that the twins were on their way before she knew of her pregnancy.

Since Darlene Jones has no record of previous ESP experiences or of subsequent ones, the unique incident concerning her twins must be explained on the basis of a reincarnation "allowance." Possibly, she was given an advance notice of her forthcoming bliss, because of a parallel situation in another lifetime where she was in some way bereft of such happy circumstances. One can only guess at the reasons for it, but the paranormal explanation is the only one that will hold water in this instance.

"Had I not been familiar with the theory of reincarnation, I would have ignored Amy-Kay," states Diane Lebo of Indiana. The unusual incident she was reporting to me concerned her two-year-old daughter by that name. The family had spent the day with friends out of town; the little girl had missed her afternoon nap and her mother knew that she would soon be asleep on the ride home. As they were riding, the mother noticed the little girl swaying from side to side in her seat and slowly getting that certain look in her eyes that came just before the child fell asleep. They were passing a familiar road now, and Mrs. Lebo said, casually, "There is the road to Nonnie's house." The word "road" must have somehow jugged the little girl's memory. Suddenly she started to mumble.

"He killed me— . . . that man killed me . . . that man killed me *in the road* . . . he killed me . . . I was born in the road and that man killed me, he stomped on me. . . ."

After this outburst, and ignoring her mother's questions, the child went back to sleep.

For a two-year-old child, such expressions seem out of place. Mrs. Lebo also noted that the child had been using strange words ever since she began to talk. For instance, instead of saying 'blanket,' she would say cover. On one occasion at the dinner table, she informed the family, "I picked cotton . . . I and mommy." Mrs. Lebo quite rightly points out that a two-year-old simply doesn't know words like born and stomped, let alone cotton.

People who have hesitated to speak out concerning the amazing exploits of their small children, did so after they saw me on television or read one of my books. Somehow I gave them courage and what seemed ludicrous on the surface of it became merely an interesting research report. Mrs. Raymond Killela, who lives in Indiana, contacted me recently to tell me some amazing things about her son Larry. "When he was around two, he would react to small one-engine-type airplanes by lying down spread-eagled on the ground. There is a small airport near our house. Whenever my husband or I were taking him for a walk and one of those small planes came overhead, Larry would react this way and then get up and resume his walk, as if nothing had happened." Apparently, the little boy only reacted this way with small one-engine planes; ordinary, large airplanes, jets, did not disturb him in the least. He would merely point at them and say, plane, like any other little boy.

However, by the time Larry reached age three things crystalized somewhat more. "He started to talk about the war with Germany, about the soldiers in their *green uniforms*," Mrs. Killela explained. "He told us, at age three, how he killed his best friend by not helping him and how he broke his leg on a large rock. He said he was taken away in a *four-passenger ambulance.* One evening we had pumpernickel bread at supper and Larry pointed at it saying it was black bread and that they ate it with fish soup. Periodically he brought up different things and made comments. We never prompted him or started deliberate conversations about it." Mrs. Killela had no idea what color uniforms the Germans wore in World War II. One day she read a book about the war and learned that the Germans wore green uniforms.

Mrs. Killela also noticed that whenever the little boy played war, as other children do, it was always the Germans and Americans. As Larry grew older, he did not refer to the things he "knew," but behaved more and more like any average boy his age. The Killelas assumed quite correctly that the four-passenger ambulance referred to by the little boy must have been a military one, and that the small one-engine planes reminded the little boy of fighter planes.

Gloria Smith who lives in New York State has a ten-year-old daughter. When the little girl was three years old, an incident

47

occurred which made Mrs. Smith wonder whether her child wasn't speaking of reincarnation memories. The family was watching television at the time and it so happened that a program dealing with Pilgrims was on the screen. Unexpectedly, the little girl said, "My *other mommie* wore clothes like that." Mrs. Smith was quite surprised and asked her daughter to repeat the statement. Firmly, the little girl replied, "The mother I used to have wore dresses like that." There wasn't anything else Mrs. Smith could get out of the child, but the little girl insisted again and again that she had had another mother and that she was dressed in clothes similar to those she was watching on television.

Mrs. H. P. Zieschang of Ohio is now well into her eighties. When she was a little girl, she frequently broke into tears and asked to go and see her *other parents.* This was a repeated occurrence, and the child, at the time, insisted that she wanted to go back to the parents *she knew.* Eventually, the desire faded as the child grew older. But to this day Mrs. Zieschang can draw a picture of her previous home and its surroundings and the little girl she used to be. Connected with this was a strong feeling of having lived in the old South. "I can't drive through certain portions of the South without looking for the one I used to live in," Mrs. Zieschang explained. "Also, one day I was standing on our porch looking out, enjoying the trees, when all at once I was standing in the doorway of a little log cabin, looking across a tiny clearing at a primeval forrest and smelling the fragrance of the trees. It was a brief flash and then I was back on my own porch."

Mrs. Tony Mazzola of St. Louis, Missouri, reported this concerning her little daughter: when Mrs. Mazzola was about five months pregnant she had a dream in which she saw herself holding a baby, not a newborn baby but rather one about five or six months old. She heard someone ask whose baby it was and answered, (in the dream) "Mine, of course." Then she heard someone ask what the baby's name was and she started to reply but could only stutter. At that moment she heard the baby speak in a clear voice, "Call me Mary." With that, Mrs. Mazzola woke up and, remembering the dream, laughed because she was quite sure that the baby would be a boy.

When the child was born, it turned out to be a girl. Mrs. Mazzola and her husband named her Rosemary. On the day when she was supposed to go home from the hospital and was waiting for her mother to take her, the sister in charge of the child entered her room and handed her a baptismal certificate listing the child's name as just Mary. The nun explained that the child had showed difficulties in breathing; the hospital staff had worked over her for forty-five minutes, and saved her. Because of the happy turn of events, they felt she should be called Mary in honor of the Madonna. The Mazzolas obliged, and Rosemary was called Mary for many years, until she went to school. Only then did she revert to the name her parents had actually picked for her.

Chapter 4
The State In Between

While it is fascinating to delve into the question of previous lives or to ferret out traces of memories with significance to the present one, such as the payment of karmic debts, it is perhaps equally fascinating to investigate the state in-between lives, the transitional period when one life on the physical plane has been terminated and another one has not yet begun. Later, I will go into the details of this system, and attempt to show how it works. In this section, however, I should like to give recent, valid examples of testimony concerning the in-between state.

In the chapter entitled, "Come Back to Scotland" in *Born Again,* I presented the case of Pamela Wollenberg of Illinois who had lived in Scotland in the early sixteen-hundreds. Under deep hypnosis the subject spoke of the experiences immediately following her death by jumping from the tower of Hunting-tower Castle. "What was your next memory after you had fallen? What is the next thing that you remember?" "I was in wind." "Did you see yourself as you were?" "Yes." "Where did you go?" "Nowhere." Following that, however, she traveled to the castle and to various places in the vicinity. As she floated through time, observing people dressed in what to her were strange clothes, she was interested only in getting back to Scotland and to the loved one she had left behind. Eventually she discovered Pamela Wollenberg who reminded her of a friend she knew in the sixteen-hundreds. Somehow she was reborn in Pamela's body. No one, at least not to her knowledge, arranged this for her nor was she told that she must go back to the physical plane.

In "the strange case of Ruth MacGuire," a chapter in the same book, the system seems to work differently, however. According to her testimony in deep trance, she stayed "on the other side" for a while, learning about her shortcomings in the life she had just left, and eventually progressed to a point where she could go back and try again. The old man who had been her teacher during that period told her that the time had come for her to go back, even though she really didn't care to. "Well, I really didn't have any choice, you know. These things are all decided," the subject explained under hypnosis. "Just what happened?" I asked. "Well, he said 'It's time now for you'; he said, 'What you do here, you've learned; you practice, you meditate, you get the right idea, the right attitude, but you can't know if you are going to make it stick until you try it in the world, and you have to try it in the world before you know whether you've really got it in your bones.'" "And how did they make you go back?" "Oh, they said, 'You have to be a baby,' and I said, 'I don't want to be a baby. There's nothing dignified in being a baby.'"

Subject then described being put to sleep, and remembered only taking some sort of dive, or rather a spin, and the next thing she remembered was crying in her present mother's arms.

N. W., a lady in Michigan, contacted me with an account of amazing clarity in which she remembered not only a previous life but also her previous death. The lady is a university graduate and had been born into a family with a very religious background. During her formative years, up to age eighteen, she was brought up on a doctrine of a strict, vengeful God, and was frequently told by her minister that she was doomed to hell because of her worldly outlook. Later, she married a young man who became a minister in the Nazarene Church. Despite this, she has always felt a rebellious spirit within her against the upbringing she was given, and five years before contacting me had begun studying other religions in order to learn more about the world she lived in. It was at the time when she had just come across the works of Edgar Cayce, that the remarkable incident occurred which prompted her to contact me.

"One day I lay down on my bed and almost immediately went to sleep," she explained, "when I found myself in a long line of slaves. In my hands was a round dish. We were walking towards the place where each slave was being served his daily ration. As I walked I kept my head lowered. I heard someone behind me whisper, 'Don't do it! He will punish you. Don't do it.' I seemed to know better than to raise my head or speak aloud to answer, but I whispered, 'I must. I just can't do what he demands of me.' The next thing I knew I was running down a tiled corridor, past two guards, in what I think was Muslim dress, through a curtain, where I saw two men sitting on cushions, deep in discussion. The guards were already advancing toward me, I tried to beg for attention and didn't succeed in being heard in the commotion. The master, the man I recognized as my master, had jumped to his feet and was berating me for interrupting him and his guest."

It should be noted that such clarity of detail is most unusual with ordinary dreams and nearly always points towards genuine reincarnation memories as the source. Mrs. W. continued her report to me, just as she remembered it the following morning.

"Next, I knew I was at the end of this corridor and I had been severely beaten and was lying there suffering terribly. I heard a noise and saw my master and his friend coming out of the room. He ordered the guards to bring me to him. They came to me, grasped my arms above the elbow and dragged me toward him. I heard myself say, 'Please, I beg of you; you're hurting me.' They dragged me to him and dropped me to the floor at his feet. I saw he had a long slender knife in his hand. I had never seen one like it before and I wondered what it was. I heard him talking to the other man but I didn't hear what he said. He then pulled me to a kneeling position, talking as he did, bent my head over, put his left arm firmly around my head while he knelt at my left side on one knee. I could feel him shaving my head at the base of the skull. I wondered what he was doing. I tried to speak. He said, 'Be quiet.' He didn't seem to be angry. Suddenly he plunged the knife into me and severed my head from my body. I screamed as he plunged the knife in and suddenly stopped. I wondered why it didn't hurt anymore and why I had stopped screaming. Then I said to myself, 'Of course it doesn't hurt anymore. I am dead.' But I could still see what was going on. He had taken the inside out of my head, the part that my present knowledge tells me was my brain, and was showing it to his guest and explaining something to him about my brain."

At that moment Mrs. W. awoke and as she did she heard herself say, "And that is why I always have migraine headaches when I'm under pressure or distressed. Now I needn't have them anymore." As a matter of fact, during the year following this remarkable dream, she has had only two headaches and both were caused by other illnesses. All through her teen-age and adult years she had suffered from one to three migraine headaches a month, until that dream, and was under medication for them. There is another thing that seems to tie in with the flashback dream. Mrs. W. has a long birthmark at the base of her skull which turns an angry red whenever she has a headache.

She is firmly convinced that the dream represents a true experience in a past life. Her husband, unfortunately, does not share her views. As a religious minister he objects to the notion of reincarnation, even suggesting that his wife might be misled by an evil spirit!

It is interesting to note that the subject had no difficulty observing the moments immediately following death. Similar description have been given by others, even those who died violently. In *The Search for Bridey Murphy* by Morey Bernstein, both the principal subject and a deceased priest report their continued and largely unchanged existence immediately following physical death. In both cases they are able to observe what goes on around them, including the funeral arrangements. Similarly, the release of the etheric body from the physical counterpart seems in no way to impede the sensory ability of the personality, proving, of course, that the seat of consciousness is in the etheric body and not in the physical shell.

Alma Bartholic lives in a small town in Texas. She is in her late forties, and was born in a small backwoods village in West Virginia. Asked to describe the environment in which she grew up, she described it as "rutted roads, narrow lanes that were tree lined like in an ancient country." When she was old enough to understand such things, her mother told her she had been born with a veil over her face, meaning with psychic leanings. As a matter of fact, Alma has at times been able to foretell the death of individuals. But she's not truly psychic in the sense that she has significant and frequent experiences. However, as far back as she can remember, she has seen a scene in her mind, which made her wonder about reincarnation. In particular, Alma wondered whether we pick our parents or are ordered by *someone* over there.

"I remember being very tired, really out of breath, as if I had worked awfully hard on something. I was sitting on something

55

soft, white and hazy like a cloud, and thinking, now that was not so very hard, but I'm glad it is over. Then a person stepped up to me and said, 'You are here,' I said, 'Yes, I just got here.' This other person said, 'Well there is someone else you have to be, you are going to another couple.' I was reluctant but this person said, 'Look down, there they are walking out that lane together.' I looked, which seemed from a great distance down. I could see them plainly. I was higher than a building, like maybe just floating in the air. I can't define this. I wasn't in an airplane until 1961, so I'm sure it wasn't a daydream."

Mrs. Bartholic wonders whether her death in one life hadn't come awfully close to rebirth into another. There was something else which seemed indicative to her of a previous life. She cannot swim in her present existence and has a distinct feeling of having drowned at one time; also, at times when she is just about half asleep she has visions of being buried alive and can even hear the dirt being thrown down on the coffin she is in. This has troubled her for many years and has given her parents some anxious moments.

If Mrs. Bartholic's life was cut short by drowning and/or being buried while not quite dead, her return to the physical world might indeed have come comparatively quickly. Being shown one's perspective parents is rare; I recall only a handful of such situations. But it would appear in this case there was some sort of need to explain the rapid return to the soul, and perhaps reassure her that she was going to some very nice people.

Bernice M. lives in Georgia. "I really do not believe I have ESP or that I am neurotic," she explained to me as she described some early incidents of a psychic nature. Since most people with authentic reincarnation memories are not generally very psychic, an exception to that assumption would be of considerable interest. At age three, Bernice saw an apparition floating towards her bedroom from another room in the house her parents then occupied. The figure wore the clothes of an earlier period, but was plainly visible to her. At age eight, her grandmother took her to visit some cousins in Pennsylvania. As she stepped into the parlor, she observed a man with white hair lying in a coffin. At the same time she noticed a sickly smell. Rushing from the room, she complained bitterly to her grandmother about being taken to a house where there was a dead man. Her grandmother assured her that there was no dead man in the house. Years later, however, her grandmother admitted that the house that she had visited used to be a funeral parlor. Undoubtedly, Bernice had psychometrically picked up an image from the past. At age seventeen, an uncle with whom she had maintained close relations passed away. Immediately after his funeral he came to her in a vision, explaining that he wasn't really dead in the conventional sense. But despite these very marked incidents involving extrasensory perception, Bernice's reincarnation memory seems undoubtedly genuine. In some ways it links up with the case reported earlier.

"The first memory I have is of being in a misty place and not looking like myself at all," she explained, "I was there with three men. I know they were not old men or young men but just men. I cannot tell you their manner of dress. I was wearing a long blue and red dress and had my hair piled on top of my head, and was very tall. I spoke to the man and asked, 'How long will I have to stay here?' They said, 'Oh, you will see, you will go back in no time.' I don't know how much time passed, but they came and told me, 'You must go back now.' I said, 'But I've only just arrived.' They said, 'We know, but it is time for you to go back.' I don't remember my birth. I do remember being about three or four months old and lying in my carriage and looking up and seeing the sky and the trees, and saying to myself, *it is true, I am alive again.*"

Just as in the previous case, Bernice M. Also has a vague memory of being dead once and lying in her coffin and, in her case, screaming at people, "I'm not dead." But they did not hear her. Since childhood, she had always known that she lived before; it seemed part of her, like breathing. When *The Search for Bridey Murphy* appeared, Bernice was about twelve years old. She could not understand why so many people denied the truth in the book. To *her* it seemed natural that everyone had lived before.

The more we understand the "period in-between" lives, the more we will understand how reincarnation works. It is clear already that every case is different and must be judged on its own merits. Yet, there are undeniable parallels in the reports coming to us from widely scattered sources, sources that have no contact with each other, no way of comparing notes, nor of discussing their individual findings with each other or with a third party. In this respect we should think somewhat more kindly of the fanciful notion found in many religions, that there is a heaven, populated by people sitting on clouds, who sometimes can look down on earth and see what goes on among mortals.

Chapter 5
Terror Cases

Some reincarnation cases have a strong ring of terror to them, that is, people go through frightening experiences, reliving incidents from the past with definite overtones of fear. Frequently, these incidents bear directly upon their present lives. Orthodox psychiatry tends to regard such material as coming from the person's own unconscious, representing unresolved difficulties perhaps, or at the very best, symbolic material, racial memories, archetypes, if the psychiatrist in question follows the Jungian line.

Terror material cannot be suppressed or ignored forever; it has a way of coming up time and again, sometimes in the dream state and sometimes while the subject is fully awake. It may be triggered by apparently totally unrelated matters, or it may simply occur spontaneously for no apparent reason. Because terror material is usually not understood as to its meaning and relationship in terms of time and spacial assignment, it can cause the subject various hardships, ranging from uneasiness under certain conditions and in certain situations to outright mental illness. As a matter of fact, I am convinced that a number of cases now diagnosed as mental illness may respond to treatment when envisioned from the perspective of possible frightening reincarnation memories. Unfortunately, medical science has as yet not reached the kind of openmindedness to experiment with such concepts on a broad basis.

Where the terror material is recognized as stemming from a possible previous lifetime, it can be dealt with. First, it must be brought to the surface by hypnosis, although conscious knowledge of it is not always desirable for the subject, while it is a necessity for the hypnotist. Once the material has been brought to the surface, at least to the satisfaction of the hypnotist, it can be analyzed. Calming material can be inserted in the unconscious mind of the subject, in order to explain that the terror of the past has no longer any bearing on the present and, possibly, suggestions that the memory of it cease altogether.

Secondly, it may be necessary, in some cases, to have the subject go through the experience from the past once again in order to act out the hidden terror, and by acting out that which has been suppressed or had disturbed the individual, exteriorize it. In this respect, the method bears some resemblance to the well-known psychodramatic technique used for disturbed individuals. All terror cases seem to be involved with abrupt death or at the very least, tragic endings. The main difference between the type of reincarnation memory I have called terror cases and ordinary flashes of memory pertaining to possible earlier lifetimes is this: ordinary reincarnation memories contain scenes of various emotional intensity, while terror cases seem to contain only the dramatic endings, the shock condition itself. Occasionally, conditions leading up to the terror are also remembered, but only in connection with it. That there is a relationship between terror cases and karmic debts I do not doubt. Of this, more in the second part of this work.

Mrs. T. Small is the only child of working-class parents, a housewife, about thirty years old and living with her husband

and two children in suburban New York City. ESP experiences run in her family, especially on her mother's side. But long before she became aware of this special talent, Mrs. Small had an odd dream which first started occurring to her when she was just seven years old and which kept recurring for some time afterwards. "I dreamt that I was at a beach and a giant wave was coming after me. I kept running but finally it engulfed the whole beach, boardwalk and town and I drowned. I've had this dream at least a dozen times and ever since have a terrible fear of the ocean." Coupled with her other ESP experiences which include precognition, one might presumably attribute this to a warning dream of something that is yet to happen. On the other hand, it has all the earmarks of a surviving memory from another lifetime as well.

Sometimes flashes into previous lives are brief, sometimes they seem to be of some duration, although in the dream state time is difficult to tell or to recall on awakening. A good case in point are the experiences of Mrs. Diane S., a housewife in her late thirties, living with her husband and three children in a small town in the Middle West. Her husband has no interest in the occult and does not believe his wife's experiences. Mrs. S. is active in her church, which happens to be Methodist; she has an interest in music and singing and is socially involved. Her interest in psychic phenomena is strictly due to her own experiences. At age twelve, she came across some books in the library which dealt with the subject of reincarnation and became fascinated by them. But soon she discovered that there was no one she could discuss her interests with. Although Mrs. S. has had a number of psychic experiences not connected with reincarnation, I do not doubt her reincarnation memories because they cannot be explained on the basis of ESP. One might, of course, consider some seemingly "ordinary" psychic experiences as also involving the karmic law in that one is compelled to follow one's hunches to make up in *this* life what one might have left undone in *another.* But this is very difficult to prove, except in the philosophical sense. Consider an experience Mrs. S. had when she was seventeen years old. She was out on a drive with her favorite boyfriend. It was getting late and he wanted to take her home, but for some reason she suddenly turned very stubborn and insisted that he take her on one more run to a certain covered bridge which stood outside their town in Ohio. There was quite an argument, since he was not prepared to do so. But Mrs. S. won out. Grudgingly, her boyfriend drove back and through the covered bridge for the second time. *At that precise moment,* a woman ran out of a ditch screaming; her clothes were half torn off her; she jerked open the door of the car and yelled that a man was trying to kill her. Her throat was covered with scratches and bruises. Naturally, the couple gave her a lift, and as they looked back they did, indeed, see a car parked close to the bank of the stream. The terrified woman explained that no other car had come by in a long time, and if they hadn't come at that precise moment, the man would have killed her. Mrs. S. wondered afterwards why she had suddenly turned argumentative and stubborn, which were not her natural character traits. Was she being impressed by a Higher Authority to come to the rescue of this woman? Was it part of a karmic relationship?

In June of 1967 Mrs. S. had a flash experience much more in keeping with traditional reincarnation. "I was about to leave my sister's house to go home, and we were standing on her front porch talking, when all of a sudden everything faded away and I seemed to be presided over by a black-robed, completely bald man. I couldn't concentrate on a single word my sister was saying and had a terrible difficulty pulling myself back to reality. But it went so fast, like a film being run very quickly. Since then, I have had several other incidents just like it, but the black-robed man was never there again. It is like a short circuit in my mind. Everything else shuts off for a fraction of a second and I get a glimpse of a picture. One time it was a girl baking a cake, another time I was looking out an open window and saw robed people carrying pitchers on their heads. Sometimes music can trigger this into happening. I was listening to music of a religious nature once, when I saw myself standing in front of a choir dressed in woven fabric like hopsacking. There were men and women in the choir. Another time I was at a window hung with heavy velvet red drapes looking across a lawn and watching someone riding to the house on a white horse."

Although Mrs. S. found she could not intelligently discuss her experiences with her family or friends, she was very much in demand as a psychic reader. She used her ability for the benefit of others, when they came to her, but sometimes wished she didn't have the talent. Among the many interesting dreams she has recorded, writing them down immediately after they happened, is one that seems to indicate a former life in some detail.

"It had to do with human sacrifice of sorts. It seems I was back in the days of the Peruvian Incas. There was a lot of red smoke, like incense smoke, clouding the scene. I was among many girls who were all there for the same thing. When it came my turn to go in, I was very frightened. They—I couldn't see them but I knew they were there—were some kind of priests, and laid me on a sort of slab, then were moving the slab toward something unpleasant. All this happened amid the red smoke. I could see myself lying on the slab, but I also was lying on the slab and looking up. I had a big feathered red, white, and blue headdress on. I was uncovered at the top and it seems that I was afraid they were going to touch my breasts and were going to hurt me. I had on a sort of girdle like you see Egyptians wearing in ancient pictures. The part that held up or was attached to the material was black and was attached to gold cloth. As I saw myself, I didn't look like I do now. I had lovely olive-colored skin and long jet-black hair. I remember at the last that the realization came to me that I was being offered to a priest as his bed partner of sorts. All the while amid the red smoke I seem to be surrounded by many people I knew to be there but couldn't see. Also, there was much drum banging and noise."

It might be interesting to see how her present "straight" life in the Middle West compares with the involuntary sexual experience she remembers from her previous incarnation. The terror of that experience must certainly have found an expression in her current life.

Josephine J. grew up in a family which believed in the occult. She works currently for a social-service organization in New York City. Five years ago her family seemed concerned about her sister, and Josephine felt that a séance might divulge some information about her sister's future. Consequently, she asked her aunt to join her for a sitting, knowing that her aunt had psychic powers. Joining her also in the sitting was a roommate. The three women sat down in the hope of receiving some sort of spirit communication or, at the very least, some psychic insight pertaining to the sister. After a few minutes of silent prayer, Josephine felt very uneasy and noticed a burning sensation in her eyes. Her aunt then became entranced by a spirit, but Josephine was unable to follow the words coming through her aunt, because she was also becoming more and more nervous, uncomfortable, and falling under the spell of the occasion. While the unknown spirit was speaking to her through her aunt, Josephine saw herself at the same time as a man wearing a pea coat and a sailor's cap, or more clearly, a captain's cap. She saw a pair of eyes staring at her, and felt she was underwater. The eyes belonged to a girl staring up at her, while she, as a man, was bending over her, holding her by the throat and keeping her underwater. While Josephine was seeing all this, the spirit continued talking to her through her aunt but Josephine was unable to understand a single word of it, being too much engrossed with her own vision and anxieties of the moment.

"Then, without realizing why," Josephine explained, "I screamed, 'I know, I know, but take those eyes off me—I'm sorry.' This I repeated over and over again, then the girl said that I had killed her. I said I knew it, that I was sorry, but that she had left me for someone else. I heard myself say, it happened not too long ago, in this century or at the turn of the century in Nova Scotia. She said, yes, and added, 'My name was Margaret and you were Anton.' Again I mentioned that she had left me, and she explained that she was younger than I and had fallen in love with a young man. On that day she had come to meet me as usual, but to tell me she would not be able to see me again, because she was going to get married. I then had become wild and grabbed her by the throat, and put her head underwater until she died."

After this horrible experience at the séance, Josephine J. tried hard to forget the incident, but could not. One day, while she was brooding over it, being alone at the time, she suddenly had a vision of a lighthouse. Somehow she knew that the man in it was herself in a previous lifetime. She could see it very clearly, standing alone on a small island, and saw herself running down a road across this island leading to a town. At the end of this road there was a house which looked more like a church or a school because it was all white with a steeple and it had a white picket fence alongside. She also knew that behind it was a cemetery. The town itself was some distance from the spot where she had killed the girl. "I saw myself, before I killed her, we were reading, sitting under a tree by a river from which I could see the lighthouse. I know I lived there once."

Josephine J. is skeptical about the entire experience. She

knows the difference between genuine mediums and false ones, and she knows the dangers of self-delusion and fantasizing. Nevertheless, the memory of having been the sailor in the pea coat is vivid and strong. There is no objective reason why she should have seen what she saw, nor is the island or landscape in the least familiar to her in her present life.

A number of terror cases seem to be connected with witch-craft or accusations of witchcraft in past centuries. This is not surprising, since those accused of witchcraft were treated about as barbarously as anyone could be treated. Nothing ever matched the furor of religious prejudice and persecution.

Mrs. Theresa L. of Kansas lives in an eighty-year-old farm-house with her five children, three horses, three dogs, one cat, and one husband; she writes novels, and enjoys traveling. Her father was in the air force, and she grew up in various countries. Her husband and she spent their honeymoon in the south of France. It was then that she had her first flashback pertaining to a possible past life. As they were driving on the road to Cahors, Mrs. L. felt compelled to tell her husband that they would shortly see a castle. Sure enough, as they rounded a curve, there was the castle standing out above the green of the trees with its golden tinted roofs. Mrs. L. wanted very much to go up to the castle, but they were too shy so they took some photographs instead. Mrs. L. was extremely disappointed and, with the passage of time, regretted even more not having gone up to that particular castle. But the incident which left its greatest impact on her, occurred when she was fifteen years old.

"I was walking down a road on the outskirts of Grigny, France. To my left was a ploughed field. For a moment, I seemed to see there a meadow, with several small trees, and one large spreading tree. It was winter, I don't know what kind of trees they were. There was a crowd of people shouting and watching while some large, one-eyed man placed a noose around a woman's neck. The scene was taking place in daylight, but the time of day was actually night. I didn't want my confessor to think I was trying to be some kind of saint, so I said nothing about it." But Mrs. L. could never pass that particular field, even before her dream experience, without feeling uncomfortable. She remembers wondering, and telling a friend that there was a witch buried there. Still, she had no sense of familiarity with the town or surrounding areas other than that particular field.

"I am female, rapidly approaching my twenty-second birthday, married a year and a half, and mother of an eight-month-old boy," explained Diane H. of Chicago in a letter to me, in which she requested my help so she could understand some very strange occult experiences. She decided to reexamine some of her dreams and visionary experiences in the light of possible reincarnation connections. Moreover, she was experiencing certain personal difficulties with her husband which could not be explained on the basis of rational thinking; there was nothing in her present life that could have caused a certain horror of sexual intercourse, yet she suspected that ever since her husband grew a beard, some sort of reflex in her caused her to connect her husband's appearance with a past-life experience involving Satanism. "I've always had a grizzly kind of fascination for Satanism," she explained; "chronologically, this dream came first. In it, I seem to be the subject of some kind of Black Mass ritual. I am aware of vague dark figures standing in a semi-circle around me. I took them to be people, but wasn't in any way actually sure that they were in any way animate. This dream was very real and in some way *familiar* to me. I was aware that if I could wake myself up, I would end the proceedings, and as I began to concentrate on this, it seemed almost as if the figures were trying to hold me there. I panicked and redoubled my efforts to wake up, which, of course, I eventually did. The panic remained for some time and I was terrified even to relax for fear I would be drawn back."

Since Diane H. had not read on or discussed the subject of witchcraft or Satanism prior to the dream, there was nothing tangible that could have triggered it. It was only a week and a half after the dream that she read *Born Again* and noticed a passage referring to Dianic Witchcraft. This triggered another discovery; since her name is Diane, she had taken an interest in the meaning of her name and discovered that the Roman and Greek goddess Diana was connected with hunt and the moon. "There were those that seemed to think she had more to do with the hunt, but I was always adamant that I was the goddess of the moon. I recall that as a child, one night on my way to bed, I was staring out the window at a full moon that was particularly brilliant. The sight really chilled me. Later that night I had a dream that somehow involved the moon. I can't remember the details, but I do recall being so terrified that for weeks after I covered my eyes when walking by a window so I wouldn't have to see the moon. It still gives me the creeps to look at it."

Diane H. is a rational and college-educated young woman and realizes she has an active imagination. "But when I consider all the small 'Satan' impressions I have had collectively, and this unreasonable fear, I wonder if perhaps they are somehow related," she explained. Admitting herself that the connection seemed far-fetched, she wondered, nevertheless, whether there might not be in a past life some experience with Satanism that would explain her current emotional difficulty in relation to her husband?

I promised to look into the matter and, if possible, relieve her of the anxiety coming between herself and her husband. Unfortunately, it wasn't until February 19, 1973, that we could finally meet at the Hampshire House in Chicago. There I had a

comfortable suite, protected from noise and unwanted telephone calls, so I was hoping that I could hypnotize Mrs. H. at
least to the first stage if not further.

I was more successful than I had hoped. After some discussion, I placed her under hypnosis and managed to get her down
to the third stage. I then brought her through several stages of
her present life to the moment of birth and past it into a
possible former life. I suggested she was present at a witches'
Sabbath, and asked her to talk about it. Finally, I hit pay dirt.

She acknowledged, under hypnosis, that she was present at a
celebration. She saw herself as a blonde and there were twelve
others with her. She said she was dancing and that there was
fire; her name was Diane and she was ten years old. I then
suggested a later period in her previous life. I commanded her to
tell me what she saw. "There is a face, a man's. He is screaming." "Where are you?" "Near him?" "Yes." "Does he speak to
you?" "Yes." "What does he say?" "You, you!" "What does he
do?" "I don't want to." "You don't want to what?" "A
stone . . . an altar . . . me . . . he's got a knife . . . he's holding
me . . . people standing all around . . . witches." "Can you see
yourself?" "Yes." She hesitated. Evidently the terror of the
experience was strong enough to prevent her from speaking
freely even in the third stage of hypnosis. Calmly, I commanded
her to tell me everything she recalled. and describe whatever
was happening to her at the time. She became very excited.
"Stop, stop. I see an altar. The place is ugly. I am afraid of him.
He wants me." "What does he do to you?" "Torture. Cuts me.
Cuts me everywhere. The ritual. A blood ritual." Immediately I
calmed her, suggesting that her fears were no longer warranted,
and that the man could not harm her. I also suggested that on
returning to consciousness she should recall the details of her
anxiety, so that reliving them once again she could get rid of
them. At the same time, as is my custom, I put in a posthyp-

notic suggestion that she would revert to her present self, forgetting everything about the past, when I uttered a certain word. I knew very well that she could not disobey my commands, having gotten her this deeply and seeing how well she had responded thus far. Shortly afterwards, I awakened her and found that she had rested well, in no way disturbed by the memories she had just encountered during hypnosis. We then proceeded to discuss what she remembered. "I was on a stone slab and there were people standing all around," she explained, "they had some kind of covering over them, you couldn't see their faces and they were standing in a semi-circle."

I asked her to describe what was done to her and by whom. "I really don't believe it was a person at all," she answered, "it was just a thing. I couldn't see it. But there was a man, an ugly face, he was trying to kiss me, he raped me." "Did you fight him?" "No, not at first. But then I remembered my husband. They tried to fight him, and he kept pulling me back. I couldn't wake up. Finally I did. I couldn't close my eyes for a while afterwards." "When I sent you back into the past, did you feel that you were that witch again?" I asked. Diane nodded emphatically. "Do you feel stronger about it now or less strongly?" "Stronger now."

The hour was growing late. I had another appointment, so I suggested that we meet again sometime in the future to continue the investigation. All along I had had the impression that Diane wasn't as relaxed as she could have been. Her husband had come along, and though I asked him to wait downstairs in the lobby, the very fact that he was in the same building may have made Mrs. H. a little nervous, especially as her husband was involved in the case, even though only indirectly.

A week later I received a letter from Mrs. H. Nothing very startling had happened since our first session with hypnosis, except that she now felt uncertain whether she had been a witch or whether she had belonged to a temple of some ancient goddess. There had been a number of dreams and shorter flashes in which she had seen herself in a temple with white pillars, open to the air and in which she wore a long white robe. She had waist-length, shiny blonde hair, which was worn straight. She remembered other little girls like her, and that they danced on a hillside, all wearing the same dresses, and learning a particular type of dance; the climate seemed very warm and someone was playing a lute. As she was trying to get names, she received something that to her sounded like Daphne or Delia. It was her impression that she had been intended to become a priestess. In some of these flashes she saw herself together with a young man and serenely happy. In another flash she saw herself older, and saying goodbye to the young man, then later being dragged away by three men, and feeling terrified. No longer dressed in white but in a "drab, dark-brown shapeless thing," with her hands bound in front and her head down, she feels she was being punished.

Next came the impression of lying on her back on a high, rectangular stone slab in a cave. The details of that horrible experience had become clearer. The man seemed to be elevated somewhat as he appeared much higher than Diane was, and he was dressed in a black robe with a chain around his neck. He had a pointed black beard. She remembers that he looked upward and raised a long bladed knife, then, holding it with both hands while he said something, he looked down at her with a sullen expression and, suddenly, he cut her body with the knife along long, thin lines, just enough to draw blood, on and on, all over her body! During this time she remembers hearing him mutter words of a ritual, but somehow it seemed a deliberate mockery on his part. She saw herself crying and moaning, which delighted the man even more. Eventually, she became aware of one final downward stab through the abdomen and then she seemed to fade away, vaguely seeing those who were standing around her dragging the body around in some kind of an orgy.

She was aware that she had died, and gradually drifted away from this scene, clutched together in one terrible hurt, as she puts it, totally drained and drifting aimlessly. Finally, she seemed to see a cluster of presences around a light, an impression she finds difficult to put into words. She relaxed for a little while, but then she had to go back, even though she did not want to and was not ready.

Her next incarnation, according to her visions, is still not her present lifetime; it appears that she has memories of having lived in Germany between 1767 and 1801. Some names rose to the surface of her consciousness, none of them capable of verification. It is her impression that she married someone named Groton and had a little boy with him who died by accident, falling down a flight of stairs. As a result, she died of the fever, lying ill for a long time. This last impression was the topic of a number of recurrent dreams which she remembers very vividly from her own childhood in *this* life.

"I was always running a fever. I'd see a seashore that was absolutely tranquil and serene, having a smooth, white, sandy shore; crystal clear calmly blue sea; and a brilliant blue sky," she explained. "There wasn't a trace of any kind of life or civilization. Then, suddenly, the entire scene would shift and the beach became terribly craggy, with sharp rocks, and enormous waves crashing against them. The sky was black. The feeling of this dream and right after it was eerie and very frightening to me. I had the dream many times, but as I grew older, it stopped."

One more impression came to her, following our meeting: Had she remained the chaste priestess she was supposed to have been, the rape in the cave would not have happened.

72

We met again in March 1973. Once again I placed her under hypnosis and regressed her to a previous life, a time when her involvement with the ancient religion had occurred. The purpose this time was to have her go through the various motions in order to externalize them from her mind. As a matter of fact, Diane obeyed my commands to pray to her goddess, and to take a few halting dance steps as she had been taught. But soon she tired, perhaps because hypnotic control away from the couch was an unusual and difficult enterprise. Consequently, I brought her back to prone position, and shortly afterwards awakened her. I heard from her again a few days later; she sounded very calm and advised me that she was well in control of her "problem." Undoubtedly, her husband's bearded appearance had innocently reminded her of the Satanic priest from her earlier existence; by bringing this to the surface and disposing of it, she removed the obstacle between herself and her husband. Thus was the terror from her past incarnation removed in the present life.

PART TWO

Chapter 6
Reincarnation and the World

What exactly is reincarnation? Now that we have discussed the subject at some length, we must come to grips with the meaning of the term. Derived from the Latin, reincarnation literally means, to enter the flesh again. The equivalent term in German, *Wiederverkörperung,* means reembodiment. Other descriptive terms include rebirth, to be born again, in German, *Wiedergeburt* (rebirth). In French, the word *renaissance* has the same literal meaning (rebirth), but is not used in the same way. Renaissance simply means a renewal of life or interest in life; a rebirth of productivity. Capitalized, it refers to renewed interest in classical art. The number of incarnations is not defined in any term; it is merely indicated that one has been born at some other time.

In the world of parapsychology we speak of discarnates and incarnates, meaning dead individuals and living individuals. A reincarnated individual has been born again in a physical body, with the understanding that some sort of memory or proof lingers on from that earlier lifetime. Basically, the idea of reincarnation involves the conviction that one may die and lose one's physical body and then return in another physical body, live another lifetime and, presumably, die again in the same manner only to return once again for any number of times. This system involves either no memory of previous lives or only partial memory of the so-called karmic law governing it. Of this more later. Reincarnation concepts should not be mistaken for two other ideas with which they are frequently confused. Anabaptism, meaning to be baptized again, is purely a religious concept prevalent among certain Protestant splinter groups. In the sixteenth century a group of religious fanatics called Anabaptists even seized the city of Münster in Westphalia and held it for a while, establishing a religiously oriented state. This state was eventually destroyed by the Bishop of Münster, and the Anabaptists were mercilessly suppressed. The French composer Giacomo Meyerbeer wrote a celebrated opera, *Le Prophète* based on this event.

In more recent times, certain American Fundamentalist communities have also practiced Anabaptism. The idea behind it is that to be baptized again, usually after one has reached adulthood, is a declaration of faith in Jesus Christ; the original baptism undertaken when the subject was a mere baby and therefore unable to grasp the significance of the act, is thus reinforced by a conscious baptism at a time when the individual is fully aware of the implications and thus can make his declaration of faith that much stronger.

Another idea frequently confused with reincarnation is *transmigration,* which refers to the passing of the soul from one state to another at death; actually, to transmigrate means to journey through an area. Transmigration signifies a possible incarnation of a human soul into animal form and, conversely, the rebirth of an animal soul into a human at a later stage of development in order to purify the soul. This philosophy, basically of oriental origin, is based on the idea that all life must undergo a gradual development up the ladder of existence. It was part and

78

parcel of the Egyptian religion in antiquity; it is still considered a valid belief by the Vedic religion of present-day India. To date, I have not found any strictly scientific evidence to support this contention. This does not mean that the concept is impossible, it only means that no factual evidence has yet turned up to support it. Probably the most valid parallel to the concept of transmigration can be found by observing the stages of the human fetus. It undergoes a rapid passing through various stages of development, including a number of animal stages. Some warmblooded animals also undergo changes from a lower order of existence to the final, higher state into which they are born. No doubt, future research will enlighten us further on this aspect of soul travel.

Reincarnation has always been viewed differently in the West than in the East. By West I mean Europe and the Americas to the extent that they were colonized by European people. By East I mean Near, Middle and Far East, and Africa. Western society, being more rationally inclined due to generic and environmental conditions, has, in modern time, generally viewed reincarnation as a subject not fit for logical discussion. Only in recent years has it become fashionable in the West to consider the possibility on a scientific basis. Western civilization, therefore, has nearly always avoided considering the impact of such a system upon its development. When there was material pointing in the direction of reincarnation, it was considered an oddity or an exception to an otherwise perfect system. If avoidance did not lead to a total sweeping under the carpet, then the problem of explaining the "unusual phenomenon" of reincarnation was relegated to religious and philosophical authorities. Most of the great philosophers of the nineteenth century viewed reincarnation with little respect. Even in our century, men who were friendly toward psychical research like Dr. Carl Jung, did not go far enough in accepting the probability of reincarnation.

If anything, the idea of "coming back as someone else" was the subject for popular jokes; in particular, the idea of coming back as an animal was held up as punishment for misdeeds in one lifetime.

A kind of transmigration is a frequent subject in Western mythology and in the wider realm of fairy stories. The idea of the enchanted prince who must live as a frog until some fair maiden saves him from his fate by being faithful runs through most Western societies. But the change from one form of existence to another was not a matter of advancing development. Rather it was a *fiat* of some supernatural authority, such as a sorcerer or a deity. Changing a human being into an animal or vice versa was reserved to those possessed of magical or superior powers.

No attempt at verification was ever made of these myths and stories. The stories were taken at face value by children, but regarded as symbolic or merely charming tales by adults. One might possibly consider them as indicative of turning the inner man into something more valuable, but I doubt that many adults look at fairy tales with such far-reaching and analytical eyes. The idea of changing a human being into something else, or an animal into a human being, is not so much an expression of the desirability of the altered state, as an expression of power, that is, the power of the one who does the enchanting. Sometimes the power to change is inherent in the position the sorcerer holds. A great magician, a wise man, a powerful king perhaps is expected to have inherent powers to do all sorts of wondrous things. An evil witch, standard character of the Western European fairy tale, also has the power to do terrible things to human beings and to animals. In her case, the power comes with the job. Others may obtain the power temporarily or on special occasions: the little boy who overhears a gnome speak the magical formula that opens the mountain, imitates it and also succeeds, only to be tripped up later by the very fact that his magical knowledge is incomplete. Or the power may be conferred on an ordinary mortal by a superior agency, such as the good fairy granting someone three wishes. In most fairy tales, magical formulas or words are used. The power inherent in *words* goes back to the very dawn of mankind, when nearly all religions considered the name of the deity sacred and possessed of great powers. In pronouncing the name of the deity (or deities) in vain, that power was dissipated and consequently the name was not spoken but covered up by the use of another term. Word magic rests largely on the belief that it works; changing from one appearance to another, from human being to animal and vice versa, is possible instantaneously, provided one knows the right words. They have to be spoken in just such a way, or at such and such a time or such and such a place, of course. Ancient magical manuscripts supplied the necessary details. In many fairy tales such special books form part of the lore.

Although the concept of transmigration as such is not anchored in Western philosophy, there is an underlying tone of changing shape under special circumstances running through all of it. In addition to the fairy tale, there are of course the horror tales, such as the werewolf traditions of Eastern Europe, and vampirism, said to originate in Romania but also strongly entrenched in Western Europe. According to these beliefs, man can change into a wolf or vampire, a blood-sucking animal, at certain times, especially when the moon is full. Actually, *lycanthrophy* is a real disease, in which an individual displays animalistic behavior due to certain disturbances of the nervous and vascular systems.

In the East, the idea of transmigration is much more firmly anchored. Even with religions in which it does not form part of the dogma, the idea of being changed into an animal occurs

81

from time to time, at the discretion of the Supreme Power. Messengers from heaven or hell or their equivalents appear in various disguises, and are capable of changing back and forth with the greatest of ease. Anyone who has ever read the *Arabian Nights,* knows of the jins or little devils, and of course, of the genie, another form of the same word. In the Tibetan pantheon alone there are several hundred demons or demigods, many of them part animal or all animal in appearance and representing various forces of nature. Similar interweaving of the worlds of man and of animals occurs in Vedic religion. Even in Buddhism and Shintoism, animalistic forms occur on occasions. However, there is no well-ordered system whereby every soul goes through various states, from low animal to human being and beyond into a divine form of existence, such as we find, for instance, in the ancient Egyptian religion. Orthodox Hindus hold such beliefs, it is true, but the caste system is still tied to individual effort and does not work equally for everybody. Just the same, in the Vedic religion we have the closest approach to orderly belief in reincarnation as we must understand it in terms of Western research. Although the Hindu accepts reincarnation as part of his religion, and on faith alone, it gives him the same comfort a Westerner might derive from scientific evidence pointint to the existence of reincarnation for all.

In the East, especially in Africa, we find belief in the return of souls into the bodies of their own descendants, such as the souls of important warriors or kings returning in the bodies of their children. These beliefs are not based on any objective research but are more in the nature of political stratagems. Similarly, the Tibetan search for the next incarnation of the Dalai Lama immediately following the death of the previous Dalai Lama, is motivated, not so much by objective research methods, but by considerations of state and religious beliefs.

When we leave the area of religion and philosophy, where,

after all, everyone may have their own ideas, ideas with which one can scarcely argue since they are essentially personal, we come face to face with the public acceptance of, and attitude toward, the reported occurrences of seemingly valid reincarnation cases. In the East, such matters are still reported in the press and in books with very little public attention, almost with public apathy. This isn't because the public lacks interest in such matters, but because, by and large, the people of the East have lived with the concept of reincarnation, and frequently also of transmigration, for so long, that any reports bearing on such subjects seem anticlimatic to them. Only among revolutionary societies, and certain government circles in present-day India, do we find active resistance to reports dealing with reincarnation material. But even in modern India, there are several universities studying phenomena of this kind in much the same way universities are studying them in the West; Professor H. N. Banerjee is probably the best known authority in this area.

Although the Soviet Union and her satellites have until recently looked with jaundiced eyes upon all psychical phenomena, research projects into ESP phenomena and all related subjects are now going on at more than a dozen universities in the Communist state. When reincarnation material occurs, it is treated with respect, although they do not necessarily reach the same conclusions a Western researcher might.

But in the free West, which includes, as I have already pointed out, the Americas, reincarnation as a serious public issue dates back only a few years. True, Swedish researchers have regressed subjects with excellent results many years before the Bridey Murphy case burst upon the public scene. But it was Morey Bernstein and his *The Search for Bridey Murphy,* which acquainted large sectors of the general public with evidential material pertaining to reincarnation.

Bernstein is the son of a wealthy manufacturer of plumbing, heating, and electrical supplies at Pueblo, Colorado. In 1953 he became interested in hypnosis and started to experiment with various subjects. As a young man of means, he did this solely out of curiosity and not because he hoped that his research would yield anything of commercial value. In his home in Colorado, and later in New York City, he pursued his studies of hypnosis and regression into former lives with a zeal that overshadowed all his other duties. Shortly after Bernstein concluded his first experiments with a housewife from Colorado, Mrs. Virginia Tighe, now known of as Mrs. Morrow, Bernstein played the tapes for me in his New York City apartment. I was impressed with both the sincerity of his efforts and the quality of the tapes, which contained much regression material concerning an alleged former life of Mrs. Tighe in Ireland.

Under hypnotic regression, Mrs. Tighe recalled in great detail her life as Bridget, or Bridey, Murphy, giving so much in the way of names, dates, and places, that Bernstein felt sure he had stumbled upon an authentic case of reincarnation. He told his findings for the first time in the *Empire Magazine,* the magazine supplement of the *Denver Post,* in 1954. The response to his article was so great that he decided to put it all into book form and, in 1956, *The Search for Bridey Murphy* was published. In the book, he protected Mrs. Tighe by giving her anonymity. This was a wise move since the book became an immediate best seller. Despite the attempt to hide her name from public knowledge, entrepreneurs managed to get through to Mrs. Tighe and offered her all sorts of opportunities, ranging from nightclub appearances to franchizing automobile agencies. Despite the documented findings, however, Mrs. Tighe does not believe in reincarnation to this day. Both she and Mr. Bernstein refused all kinds of offers, preferring the rational, scientific approach to the problem. They did, however, permit Paramount to make a movie based on the book. In the motion picture Teresa Wright played Mrs. Tighe, and Louis Hayward, Bernstein. Part of the payment received for the motion-picture rights went to the subject. The motion picture was a flop, perhaps because it treated the book with less than sincerity and respect.

Today, if you ask an average person whether they remember Bridey Murphy, the majority will answer, "Yes, but wasn't that proved to be a hoax?" This, if nothing else, proves the old Roman saying, *semper aliquid haeret* meaning "something always sticks." No matter how great a lie or smear, no matter how unfounded, people will remember it even if it has later been proven false. Thus it was with the book. Although it is not generally known, a major picture magazine tried to buy rights to the story from Mr. Bernstein. The author did not like the terms and refused the offer. Shortly afterwards, the same picture magazine sent a team of investigators to look into the background of Mrs. Tighe. In the Middle West they came up with what they claimed to be proof of Mrs. Tighe's Irish background. From bits and pieces, neighborhood conversations, hasty conclusions concerning her acquaintanceship with an Irish priest, the picture magazine constructed a story the gist of which was that the "reincarnation memory" was actually due to her childhood memories when she knew Irish people in her immediate environment. So contrived was this "explanation," and so patently motivated by the earlier rejection of a sale to the same magazine, that Mr. Bernstein's hometown paper, the respected *Denver Post,* found the money and personnel to put together an investigative team of their own. The *Denver Post* team, however, went all the way to Ireland to check out the original story in painstaking detail. The result was that the *Denver Post* published a six-part series concerning the Bridey Murphy case, in which not only was all of Mr. Bernstein's original findings corroborated, but much new material was added to it, upholding the reincarnation theory.

Later on, the new material was incorporated into a reissue of the book itself and in the paperback version which came out in 1970. At that time, Morey Bernstein spent part of the year in Miami. As a result of the renewed interest in the story, Bernstein and his star subject were interviewed again in the press and on television. "Writing *Bridey* was the most important thing I've done in my lifetime," Bernstein is quoted as saying. Bridey Murphy was born in Cork in 1798 and died in Belfast in 1864. There were six sessions altogether. "Today the book is taken seriously by psychic researchers and enjoying a new popularity. It has been called a parapsychological classic and its principals are finally able to laugh at its debunkers," says Bob Wilcox, the *Miami News* religion editor. Nowadays, Morey Bernstein commutes between his winter home in Colorado and his summer home in Florida, is knee deep in the investment business, and planning to write two more books.

Despite the fact that in the popular mind, especially in America, Britishers are likely to believe in ghosts, live in haunted castles, and are supposed to be very friendly towards all sorts of psychic phenomena, the truth is quite different. Due to the fact that England is a very densely populated country, Britain does have a larger amount of psychical occurrences than more sparsely settled countries. But the public attitude toward such phenomena is by no means as friendly as Americans are sometimes led to believe. If anything, it is more likely to be favorable amongst the lower income groups and the lower social strata than in the educated or scientifically minded part of the population. Reincarnation, generally considered part of the occult field, has even less of a chance to be treated seriously in England. While the public and some scientists may take a certain interest in phenomena of this kind, the British press, by and large, is not only hostile to all kinds of ESP phenomena but goes to great lengths, or perhaps I should say depths, to debunk them, and sometimes invents angles that will make the phenomena appear fraudulent. Compared to the American attitude, which is not exactly positive in this respect either, the British press is many times worse.

It was therefore a distinct surprise to see reincarnation material reported quite fairly and accurately in a leading British newspaper. It all started with Ada Kay, a sometime actress and a sometime writer, who now makes her home in Scotland. Long before I met the tall, dark-haired lady in Edinburgh, I was told of her unusual experiences and memories of another life by my good friend Elizabeth Byrd, the American author of *Immortal Queen* and *Flowers of the Forest.* Elizabeth met Ada for the first time in April 1970. At that time Elizabeth expressed some frank doubts concerning the validity of Miss Kay's story. Miss Kay believed herself to be the reincarnation of the Scottish king, James IV. This was the unfortunate king who lost a vital battle and his life to Henry VIII of England in 1513. The corpse was later decapitated by a pair of careless soldiers. Between 1970, when Elizabeth first met her, and a recent visit to Scotland I made in April 1973, Elizabeth and many of her friends among Scottish writers had become thoroughly convinced of the genuineness of the phenomenon. By now Miss Ada Kay, who prefers to be called A. J. Stewart (she was married briefly), lives in a friend's house in the best part of Edinburgh. There she spends her days thinking how she can help Scotland regain its independence from England, doing some writing, of course, and receiving her many friends and admirers. She is firmly convinced that she *was* James IV, and fancies herself a kind of Scottish Joan of Arc, waiting for the call to help Scotland free itself from "foreign" domination.

What brought her to general attention in England and Scotland was a superbly written book, *Falcon,* which told the story of the unlucky King James IV of Scotland in amazing detail. One might argue that a careful researcher could have come up with much of the material, but there are large sections in the book which seem to defy historical research. The Scottish press has always been more kindly inclined toward phenomena of this kind than their English breathren. In the *Scottish Sunday Express* of February 15, 1970, Graham Williams says of Miss Kay, "Miss Kay had been commissioned to write a play about the king. Gradually the influence of James IV took hold of her. Then she visited friends in the south of Scotland and was told that they were going to visit Flodden Field the next day. She awoke screaming in the middle of the night, dreaming that she was being killed by English soldiers. A friend rushed into the room and after hearing her description of what had happened said simply, 'You *are* James IV.' "

Gradually, more and more material about the life and times of James IV started to emerge from her memory. As she wrote the book, it seemed as if it were being dictated by some superior force within her. Miss Kay is quoted as saying, "This book has been an endurance test. I did not want to write it, but I was forced to. It came out in a rush of words, dates, names, references and things of which I should have known nothing had I not been James IV."

But the publication and success of *Falcon,* at least in England, was by no means the end of Miss Kay's role as the reincarnated James IV. In fact, it was only the beginning.

When I saw her in 1973, her main concern was to find her "James bones." She recalled quite vividly that her body had been left in a little chapel not far from the battleground, and that two soldiers had cut the head off. That much, of course, can be traced in historical records, as she's quick to admit. Where the mystery begins is what happened to the rest of the skeleton. It has become a kind of obsession with her to find the burial place of the rest of "her bones." For that reason she requested that I regress her to find out what happened to her bones. I agreed, and upon my arrival in Edinburgh, we arranged for a meeting the following evening. Picture my surprise when I arrived at the stately house where Miss Kay was staying as the permanent guest of a friend, then living in London. Stretched out on a chaise longue was the tall former BBC writer, resting on one elbow, dressed in a steel-gray, long gown with a chain belt. She was surrounded by about ten friends who were anxious to see what could be learned from the hypnotic experiment. Among them was Dr. David Stevenson, a lecturer at Edinburgh University, who is friendly toward Miss Kay and the phenomenon, although by no means convinced of its genuineness.

The dramatic setting did not help the success of the venture. Try as I might, Miss Kay did not "go under." I realized that the large number of eager observers weren't going to help me and suggested another time when Miss Kay and I could meet alone. This was readily agreed upon and I tried again. Once more, the experiment was a total failure. It then occurred to me to discuss her case with her in frank terms. Quite obviously, I felt, the sex change in the purported present incarnation might have caused certain personal problems in her. The question was, did her change from male to female in this life bring with it certain sexual imbalances in her own behavior, or were her present difficulties due to having been a man in a previous lifetime?

The James IV incarnation was by no means the only reincarnation memory she could come up with. Although my hypnotic regression was not a success, I did manage to get her under to the first stage during our first meeting. At that time, though fully conscious, she spoke of life as a German prince, and named Prince Ruprecht of the Palatinate as a person she either was or knew in that lifetime. Her personal interest, however, lay not in that incarnation but in the Scottish one. Consequently, she did not want to go any further in a direction which, to her way of thinking, would not lend itself to what she was after; proving once more that she was, indeed, James IV of Scotland. At our private meeting I made it clear that I could not judge the factuality of her Scotish incarnation at this point; too much research had gone into the matter, too many imponderables had to be considered. On the face of it, her reincarnation memories indicated life at the time of James IV, that much I was convinced of. Whether she was indeed the unlucky monarch, was another matter, but again, I felt very strongly that she was. What disturbed me, however, and I was frank in pointing it out to her, was her insistence on *continuing* the life of James IV in this incarnation instead of being merely Ada Kay and living her own life. I suggested that she accept her previous incarnation as King James IV, do everything in her power to speak of him in her writings, but that being done turn to her own pursuits and develop herself as a writer on other subjects as well. Certainly, A. J. Stewart's book, *Falcon*, belongs with *The Search for Bridey Murphy* as a classic on reincarnation.

As soon as the public furor over Ada Kay (A. J. Stewart) had reached its zenith, other cases of reincarnation came to the surface. None of them, to be sure, were as spectacular in their implications as Miss Kay's. But the *Scottish Daily Express* started to run an entire series entitled "Reincarnation—Have *You* Been Here Before?"

There was, first of all, Derric St. Julian-Bown, a consultant designer living near London. He distinctly remembers marching across the Alps as part of the main army of Charles VIII of France. A certain scene has haunted him all his life. As an artist he was able to draw it. The scene contained a woman pulling on the handle of a locked door, and below, on the stairs, there is a man with a crossbow at his shoulder. Passing through the Mont Senis pass between Italy and France he experienced the strong impression that he had been there before. Gradually bits and pieces of the past started to surface in his memory. He knew then that he had been born in 1472 as a Scotsman named Angus MacCullum, in a village named Colgin, near Oban. The village no longer exists, but it did exist in the fifteenth century. Mr. Bown remembered the name of the woman he met and married in the fifteenth century, he remembered the places they visited together and even how he died. All this was later checked out and found to be authentic.

Another case selected for publication by the *Scottish Daily Express* because it had the ring of truth to it concerned a man named Oliver Weller. Mr. Weller, in trying to think back as far as he could in this life, as a game with a friend, suddenly remembered a previous lifetime. He remembered it so well, that he knew who he was, where he lived, who his wife had been, what he and she had died of. He was also able to describe several buildings in the town in which he had lived in his previous life. With the friend, he set out to the town of Midhurst, where he felt he had lived and died in 1891. Sure enough, they found the landmarks, the buildings Mr. Weller had described although he had never been to Midhurst in his life, that is, not in this one. According to the story in the *Scottish Daily Express* of May 5, 1970, Mr. Weller stated that he had lived as a railroad worker named Charles Edwards in Midhurst and had died of a heart attack. He also knew that his wife was named Jane and had died of paralysis in 1891. The two men managed to find the records in the local registry office—of both Charles and Jane Edwards— and discovered that Jane Edwards had indeed died of paralysis in 1891. In another set of records they found that Charles Edwards, laborer, had died of cardiac disease. Unless Mr. Weller had faked the entire story, and he patently had not, there simply is no other explanation than reincarnation.

The series continued with the account of a Colonel William Blakeney, a professional army officer, not given to fantasies or hallucinations. He has distinct memories of having been a soldier in India during the time of Clive in the eighteenth century, and of having been executed by being thrown off a high cliff. He remembered much of this when he visited locations connected with these eighteenth-century events as part of his official mission in India, even though he had never been to the particular places previously nor had any knowledge of their history.

The *Scottish Daily Express* also presented the strange case of Edward Ryall, who had been aware of memories outside his present lifetime ever since he was a teenager. As John Fletcher, he felt he had died of a blow to his skull during the battle of Sedgemoor in 1685. Proof of his earlier lifetime came to Mr. Ryall gradually. He had always used words which were strange to his native Essex. But when he passed the site of the battle of Sedgemoor on a holiday in 1960, everything fell into place for him. He remembered his previous name, and how he died during the rebellion by the Duke of Monmouth. Although Mr. Ryall in his other identity as John Fletcher did not want to become a rebel, he was persuaded by friends to help them in battle. He went on a scouting expedition with his friends and was caught by a horseman. "The last I heard was a swishing, whistling sound," Mr. Ryall is quoted, "then there was a great red flash in my head and after that . . . nothing."

There were several statements Mr. Ryall had made that convinced not only journalists but scientists as well that his case was a remarkable one and evidential for reincarnation. Although he had never been to the area of the battle before, he had frequently spoken of *rhines,* pronouncing the word as "reen." These, he had stated, were drainage ditches. In his native Essex the same ditch is called a dyke. Mr. Ryall had also said that the year before the battle there had been a very severe winter, and that the local church had an open staircase running up the inside of the wall. On checking it out, it was discovered that the winter from 1683 to 1684 had been unusually severe in the area, and that the church at the local village did indeed have such a staircase, although it had long been enclosed.

The religious establishment has viewed reincarnation with various attitudes. In the past, any deviation from the norm was considered heresy. People were persecuted for it more in the West than in the East, but, in essence, no established churches like their followers to have doctrinal ideas of their own. In the West, early Christianity contained elements of beliefs in reincarnation. This may be due to the Essene influences which showed in the teachings of Jesus because of his background as a student at the Essene monastery at Quumram.

When Christianity became a state religion and the early concepts were edited to fit in with this new view of the faith, much early material was deliberately omitted or suppressed. Not only were several Books of the Bible removed, but passages intimating belief in reincarnation were also taken out or rewritten in subsequent translations. From about 300AD onward, Christianity was no longer identical with the early teachings of Jesus, but had become a combination of his teachings with later religious philosophical thought and the necessities of an emerging state religion. The medieval church had no use for reincarnation. Belief in the Final Judgment, a moment when the dead are called to account for their sins on earth, is a cornerstone of Christian dogma. If man were to go through a succession of lives, without that Final Judgment Day much of the power of the faith would have been lost. The church needed the whip of Judgment Day to keep the faithful in line. It was therefore a matter of survival for the church not to allow belief in reincarnation to take hold among her followers.

For somewhat different reasons, the Jewish religion does not like the idea of reincarnation either, even though there are hints of it in Scriptures. Notably, the Prophet Elijah, was always expected to come again and this idea can even be found in early

Christianity. But the Hebrew faith rejected the idea of reincarnation since it would indicate a system in operation that was not wholly dependent upon the grace and will of a merciful God. A personal God was very much at the heart of both Hebrew and Christian faiths in the beginning. Only in later years has the moral concept of religion become a stronger focal point.

Some Protestant faiths, especially of the Fundamentalist persuasion, put their emphasis on Jesus Christ as the personal savior of mankind. Consequently, a law that applies universally to all men and gives them rebirth regardless of this personal savior is particularly odious to the Fundamentalist.

Some great religious leaders say one thing but their followers understand another. Emanuel Swedenborg was an eighteenth-century scientist, philosopher, and seer in Sweden. Among his proven accomplishments is a detailed description of the great fire of Stockholm which he described to a number of witnesses while some seventy miles away from it. Swedenborg did not found a new religion in his lifetime; his many books, among which *Heaven and Hell* is perhaps the best known, were later used as the foundation for a religious faith called simply The New Church. It has many followers in Scandinavian countries and in this country especially in Minnesota, where many immigrants from Northern Europe settled, but also in various other parts of the United States. A cornerstone of this religion is a belief in the coming of a "New Jerusalem."

The writings of Swedenborg indicate quite clearly that he had visions in which he saw "the other side of life" very much the way spiritualists do and almost the same way scientists feel who follow the "survivalist" line in parapsychology. The terminology may differ, but, in essence, Swedenborg speaks of a number of "societies" where people live after physical death. Depending upon the state of consciousness prior to death, one joins a particular society and advances to a higher one when one is ready to do so. The Swedenborgians in the United States are,

94

by and large, a peaceful lot and not given to missionary efforts. It was therefore with some surprise that I received a note from Duncan Brackin of Minneapolis, an avid Swedenborgian, wondering how I could possibly lean toward reincarnation. "Swedenburg proved reincarnation to be an error once and for all for those who have eyes to see," Mr. Brackin complained. He sent me a little pamphlet entitled *Reincarnation—The View of The New Church.* As far as rebirth is concerned, the Swedenborgian church accepts only spiritual rebirth, and that during the earthly life of man and mostly while he's not even aware of it.

Among modern churches, the Episcopal Church and some of the liberal Christian churches, such as the Universalist and Unitarian faiths have been most receptive to material hinting at the reality of reincarnation. They see no conflict of unsurmountable proportions in the teaching of reincarnation and their own concepts. As long as man accepts the teachings of Jesus, they feel that it does not matter whether he lived once or several times. Very few Catholic priests and layman will commit themselves on the subject of reincarnation. Those who are openminded toward it are quite unusual. The problem here lies with fundamental issues: if psychic phenomena are accepted as natural and realistic happenings, the entire basis of the miraculous story of Jesus could be explained entirely on the basis of psychical research. This would, on the other hand, make the miraculous side of it far more acceptable to sophisticated individuals who do not accept their religion on faith alone, but, on the other hand, it would deprive the account of the resurrection of its uniqueness. It is precisely that uniqueness which the church needs so sorely to build her entire edifice upon.

Nothing reported about Jesus, both while in the body and after his physical death, is inconsistent with the findings of modern parapsychology. As a matter of fact, parallel happenings have been reported from many other quarters. Perhaps

95

none of them were quite as spectacular or had such fortuitous dissemination, but psychical healing, materialization and de-materialization, levitation, and finally, the appearance of a person known to have died after physical death are well-attested phenomena which have occurred, from time to time, in the annals of psychical research all over the world. What makes the position of Jesus unique, therefore, is not the phenomena as such but the *implication* of the phenomena and, of course, Jesus' teachings and views. The phenomena themselves, in my opinion, were used by Jesus consciously and deliberately to underscore his belief in the continuance of life after death. Whether Jesus was, in fact, a believer in reincarnation cannot be ascertained with certainty, especially since so many of his sayings and teachings have been lost, or were perhaps eliminated at later dates. But there was a belief among Jesus' contemporaries that he had come as the reincarnated prophet Elijah, and a much-quoted exhortation, "to live, you must be born again" may be a hint at reincarnation beliefs. Much of Jesus' philosophy was misunderstood even at the time when he promulgated it. His references to his "Father," his assertion that his Kingdom was not of this world, "judge not lest ye be judged" are all indications of symbolic language and were, I think, not to be taken literally.

Although we are moving toward greater enlightenment in religion, and a much more flexible attitude on the part of the various religious establishments, we have as yet not come to grips with the problem of integrating scientific findings into the religious edifice, especially when such findings go counter to traditional doctrine. When the various religious establishments realize that there lies strength in incorporating scientifically supported findings of this kind into their philosophies, they may very well regain their following, especially among the young, which they are losing more and more daily.

Chapter 7
Reincarnation and Science

"The evidence indicates that reincarnation is a fact. I think it likely that people have been born before and that after they die will be born again on this earth." This is the headline-making quotation in an article on reincarnation in the popular weekly, *The National Enquirer*. This weekly newspaper is not known for its subtlety of approach, nor necessarily for the reliability of its information. But in recent times the *Enquirer* has abandoned a hardcore policy of scandal and violence for a large percentage of headline-making news from the field of parapsychology, astrology, and the occult in general. As a result, its circulation has risen to even greater heights than before.

The above quotation is not from some metaphysical believer, or astrologer, or amateur investigator. It is the expressed opinion of Dr. Ian Stevenson, head of the Department of Neurology and Psychiatry at the University of Virginia's School of Medicine. Dr. Stevenson has for many years been the champion of reincarnation research in the United States. His first book on the subject, *Twenty Cases Suggestive of Reincarnation* was soon followed by additional material which he published through the American Society for Psychical Research, and another book of additional cases is now in preparation. Stevenson has investigated cases both in the West and in the East and has done so on a careful, scientific basis. No one can rightly accuse Dr. Stevenson of being a charlatan, or of jumping to conclusions. His language is careful and he makes no unjustified claims. The difficulty toward total acceptance of his findings, and the findings of others like myself, which parallel them, lies in the stubborn insistance on the part of most orthodox scientists that laboratory experiments are the only way of proving reincarnation. "Nobody has as yet thought up a way that reincarnation could be proved in a laboratory or a test tube," the professor is quoted in his interview. In studying hundreds of valid reincarnation cases he had used the methods of the historian, lawyer, and psychiatrist in combination. Gathering testimony from as many witnesses as he could, he and his staff sometimes interviewed as many as twenty-five people regarding a certain case. Sometimes he goes back for further interviews, if the original talk has not been satisfactory or conclusive. Everything is being taken into account; the behavior of the person who claims to have lived before, the environment in which he lives, his background, education and general knowledge and even his personal habits. "Many of those claiming to have lived before are children. Often they are very emotional when they talk of the person they used to be and they can give minute details of the life they lived," Dr. Stevenson added.

Dr. Stevenson, just as any responsible parapsychologist does, always looks for alternate explanations so that he may rule them out, before he accepts reincarnation as the answer to a puzzling case. Everything is considered; early experiences, accidental information, newspaper accounts, anything that might have been forgotten consciously but can be brought out under hypnosis. Fraud, memory lapses, fantasy, and wishful thinking have all got to be considered and eventually ruled out before a valid case for reincarnation can be established, according to Dr. Stevenson's method of inquiry. But that is by no means the end. He explained that he has also got to consider and exclude telepathy as a means of obtaining unusual information. "Extrasensory Perception cannot account for the fact that the subject has skills and talents not learned, such as the ability to speak a foreign language without having had the opportunity to learn it in this present life."

Although most of the cases investigated by Dr. Stevenson were in India and the East, he has also looked into some interesting situations in Alaska and Europe. This is not because fewer cases occur in the West, but because the prevailing attitude of the public makes discovery of such cases more difficult. In the East, the climate is more favorable towards a free and open discussion of such matters; in the West, only very courageous people dare come out with statements that they may have lived before.

The author of the *Enquirer* article, Doug Laurie, then asked Dr. Stevenson whether reincarnation might not explain child geniuses such as Wolfgang Amadeus Mozart or Alexander Hamilton. Mozart was an accomplished musician and composer before the age of ten; Alexander Hamilton had almost no formal education, yet could speak French fluently before the age of twelve. Dr. Stevenson allowed that the incidence of child genius cases might be attributable to reincarnation.

The article then quoted in some detail half a dozen cases investigated by Dr. Stevenson and by a colleague of his, the already mentioned Dr. H. N. Banerjee of India, all of them completely proven in every detail. Those among my readers who wish to acquaint themselves with these verified cases of reincarnation, may find the rather lengthy accounts of the investigations in the books of Dr. Ian Stevenson and Dr. H. N. Banerjee.

New evidence and new cases suggesting reincarnation turn up constantly. The New York *Daily News* of January 9, 1971, told of Alfonsito Weshner, age four, as the star of discussions with college professors in Montreal. "Alfonsito amazed the educators with general knowledge and his special interests music and the arts."

Old-line scientists prefer to regard reincarnation research as exotic and reject the evidence out of hand without ever examining it. Some parapsychologists, even conservative ones, are eager to examine what material there is, especially since Dr. Stevenson has opened the door to such investigations. The acceptance of reincarnation as a reality is a hard nut to swallow for some. Inevitably, it means simultaneous acceptance of survival after physical death. Some parapsychologists still cannot accept that probability, simply because they have been weaned on laboratory research methods and cannot or do not wish to understand that the evidence is in the *field*, among spontaneous phenomena or actual, unplanned occurrences.

The material for the survival of human personality is overwhelming, far more so than the evidence for reincarnation. Strangely though, some support for reincarnation research can be gotten among scientists who, on the surface, would be the least likely interested in such a subject. I am speaking here of physicists and physical scientists. The reason is that in learning about the nature of energy and mass, and in dealing with the electromagnetic forces in the universe, many of these scientists have come to realize that energy is indestructible. Basing their views to some extent on Albert Einstein's pioneering opinions, they, too, feel that energy may be transformed into other forms of power or into mass, but can never be dissipated entirely. Since the life force, the human personality, is an energy field, they argue that such fields cannot be dissipated either and must therefore *continue to exist in some form.* Experiments involving

100

the discovery of energy fields in so-called haunted locations and of significant changes in the atmosphere of an experimental chamber, such as ionization, have been going on for some time. It is therefore not too surprising that such strong centers of technical learning as the Newark College of Engineering and the New York Institute of Technology (where I teach) should be interested in parapsychology, and within that field, reincarnation research.

Medical science has been more hostile towards reincarnation material than any other branch of science. This may be due to the fact that medical science relies heavily upon the assumption that man is essentially a physical being. As Dr. William McGary, the brilliant physician working in conjunction with the Association for Research and Enlightenment in Phoenix, Arizona, has pointed out to me on a recent visit, the basic difference between orthodox medical science and medicine based upon such knowledge as the Edgar Cayce records, lies in the way they regard the human being. To conventional medicine, man is structural, that is to say, the physical body is the essence of man and mind is merely a subdivision thereof. To the esoterically oriented person, man is functional, not structural. The physical person is a manifestation of spirit or mind which came first, and represents the outward expression of the soul that governs and determines everything from within. Such thinking is at variance with conventional medical procedure, of course, since it necessitates the treating of illness from a total point of view rather than from the usual sectional or physical viewpoint.

For a medical doctor to accept reincarnation as a reality necessitates changes in his medical approach as well; except for the psychiatrist, the conventional physician has little to do with the nonphysical aspects of human personality. The general practitioner and the specialist both leave mental problems to the psychiatrist, concentrating on purely physical problems.

101

Thus the question of reincarnation research becomes essentially one of acceptance or rejection by the psychiatrist and psycho-analyst. Today, the majority of psychiatrists explain any valid reincarnation material as malfunctions of personality, ranging all the way from mild neuroses to schizophrenic conditions. Just as the conventional analyst will regard *all* dream material of his patient as purely symbolic and representative of suppressed material in the unconscious part of the mind, so the psychiatrist will explain reincarnation memories either as aberrations of the mind, or, if the particular psychiatrist is a Jungian, as racial memories, or archetypes.

But these scoffing psychiatrists and analysts seem to forget that Dr. Sigmund Freud, the father of modern psychiatry, himself leaned toward parapsychology in the later years of his life. He made the statement in print that he would want to study parapsychology, if he had to do it all over again. One of his star pupils, Dr. Carl Jung, who has contributed as much to psychiatry as Freud, was not only firmly convinced of the reality of psychic phenomena but possessed ESP himself. His discovery, or if you prefer, invention of the *archetypes* as a symbolic expression of "original concepts" does not militate against genuine reincarnation experiences, in his view. At the Jung Institute in Zurich, much research went on in this area in the 1930s and 1940s. In his important work, *Acausal Synchronicity (The Law of Meaningful Coincidence),* Jung postu-lates that there is a superior order of things, connecting events and people. This superior order lies beyond the law of cause and effect and must be dealt with on different terms. What Jung is hinting at in this precedent-shaking work is the existence of a law of fate; by trying to explore the ways in which this noncausal link seemed to work, Jung approached the question of fate, free will, and reincarnation, which is intimately con-nected with them, in a modern, scientific way for the first time.

Some years ago, the late Eileen Garrett, world-renowned

medium and president of the Parapsychology Foundation, accompanied Dr. Robert Laidlaw, psychiatrist and head of a department of psychiatry at Roosevelt Hospital, New York City, to a number of mental institutions in order to discover whether some of the inmates might be suffering from genuine cases of possession. The very fact that a reputable medical doctor would even attempt to undertake such an expedition is a step forward beyond belief. Dr. Laidlaw never made any claims of wholesale acceptance of the tenets of parapsychology. But he did accept that which, in his view, had been proven without reservations. He engaged himself in research dealing with psychical healing and has shown a great deal of interest in cases of hauntings and ESP in general. It was Dr. Laidlaw who conducted the investigation with me when the late New York *Daily News* columnist Danton Walker invited us to his haunted house in Rockland County. Laidlaw has an open mind on reincarnation; he is actively working with the American Society for Psychical Research and other bodies in accumulating facts pertaining to reincarnation that may yield a better understanding of the system by which it works.

In the spring of 1973 I obtained permission to visit a lady named Verna M. in a state hospital in the state of Georgia. She had been in and out of mental hospitals, confined generally as a case of schizophrenia. For some time prior to my visit, she had maintained that she remembered previous lifetimes. It was her contention that a full exploration of those earlier existences might help her understand her present predicament. I was her last hope, and even though she knew that I wasn't likely to come to central Georgia just to see her, she wrote to me in great despair. Apparently she was rational most of the time, lapsing into fits of schizophrenia, and refusing to cope with life on the outside at certain intervals. At such times she was committed to or committed herself voluntarily to medical supervision.

It so happened that I had some business in Atlanta and

arranged with Mrs. M. to visit her at the state hospital. Obtaining permission and even cooperation of the medical authorities at the state hospital was a remarkable accomplishment in itself. The institution turned out to be a modern, well-kept mental facility in rural central Georgia. The therapists and the supervising medical doctor greeted me with great cordiality.

I proceeded to interview Mrs. M., first in order to ascertain the details of her conscious memories. I was able to find certain inconsistencies in her narrative, inasmuch as reincarnation as an explanation was concerned. I discovered, for instance, that she had had a number of valid ESP experiences and also that she very definitely suffered from personality problems. Under hypnosis, which was undertaken by me on a kind of stage so that it could be taped for internal television, Mrs. M. proved to be an excellent subject and rapidly went to the third stage of hypnosis. I was able to discover some suppressed material concerning her own father, and other details which had not been known to the hospital authorities. Prenatal regression yielded nothing. But through hypnosis I discovered that the entity Mrs. M. had thought was *herself* in a previous incarnation, was in fact a discarnate individual who had attached herself to Mrs. M. in order to continue expressing herself. Thus, the supposed case of reincarnation turned out to be one of possession.

Upon bringing her out of her hypnotic state, I explained some of this to Mrs. M. and, as a result, she learned to accept conditions in her life as they are, no longer relying on previous incarnations and unfulfilled hopes as crutches which eliminated the need to stand on her own two feet in *this* life. Mrs. M. has since left the institution and returned to private life.

Whether or not conventional scientists will accept reincarnation research in the foreseeable future, the work will go on with even greater emphasis as time passes. Even in Russia, studies in reincarnation are now being undertaken. The rate of progress in the Western world will depend on the availability of trained investigators, good hypnotists, and of course good research facilities to back up the investigators. There is no dearth of promising subjects; the small selection mentioned in the first part of this work should give an indication of the available material. However, people without overt memories or other substantial indications of previous lives should not be put under hypnosis merely in the hope of finding previous lives. If reincarnation research were to be based solely on hypnotic regression, the outlook would indeed be grim. Even Dr. Ian Stevenson does not regard regression through hypnosis as the major factor in his research. As a follow-up method it is valuable and frequently yields excellent results. As the initiator of reincarnation research, it is frequently useless and sometimes deceiving. Spontaneous, unsought occurrences are still the backbone of all valid reincarnation material.

Chapter 8
The Law of Karma

"Karmic relationship" and "paying off old Karma" are terms bandied about frequently among esoteric people (those who are interested in the occult and psychical research and in astrology). But the average person doesn't quite know what the term Karma means. The word itself comes from India and signifies something like "accumulated destiny." Possibly there is a link between the Indian term Karma and the Greek idea of caritas, derived from Karys, the goddess of charms and destiny. Words like caring, care, charity, charm, charisma, the technique called Charismatics (an idea created by me) may be interlinked, if not in meaning, then in derivation.

But Karys was also the goddess of the occult, of certain aspects of the underworld, and as such, ruled man's fate. Any discussion of reincarnation is impossible without reference to the Karmic Law. It is that law which governs the nature of each incarnation. The Karmic Law is the set of rules under which the system called reincarnation operates. It is not a law in the sense of human laws, with judges and lawyers arguing back and forth the merits of each case. Under the Karmic Law there are no appeals and no interpretations that may differ from interpreter to interpreter. The Karmic Law is more comparable to a law of nature, such as the law of cause and effect, the law of attraction and others found in the existing universe.

There are no exceptions from natural law; what seems at times a breach or circumvention of natural law is merely an aspect of it that we haven't fully understood. In time, we will understand such strange workings of natural law to the point where they are no longer strange to us. I am speaking here particularly of some psychic phenomena which are seemingly in contravention of conventional physical law, but are in fact merely extensions of it in areas where we do not possess sufficient knowledge.

The Karmic Law has several important aspects. It operates impersonally, regardless of who may be involved. Since it plays no favorites and is not emotionally tinged in any way, it cannot be manipulated to favor one or the other. The Karmic Law is not written in text books or contained in physical reference files. It exists, beyond time and space, in an orderly fashion, it has existed from, I don't know when, and it is referred to in many cultures at various times, independent from each other, and yet no one has ever seen its scrolls. About the nearest thing to an orderly "filing system" are the so-called Akashic records. These records are said to contain the destiny and accumulated lives of everyone on earth, past, present, and future. The great seer Edgar Cayce refers to them in his trance readings, and lesser prophets have had reference to the Akashic records whenever they give so-called "life readings."

While I have my doubts about the ability of some modern psychics to consult these records at will and extract information regarding former lives for individuals, I cannot help but wonder whether the great Edgar Cayce may not indeed have been right in stating that these records exist. There seems to be an actual need for some sort of central clearinghouse if man's destiny is an orderly process. The Karmic Law would be very difficult to administer if some sort of record were not kept of the individual's deeds in each incarnation. Thus, while I cannot say that I know where these records exist, I feel that they may well be a reality in the nonphysical world. Interestingly enough, Tibetan tradition speaks of a similar record in existence in a remote monastery in Tibet, where every person's life is recorded and where previous incarnations are also listed. If such a book exists on the physical plane, no trace of it has yet been found, but then there are many things which exist of which we know nothing *as yet.*

How do you acquire Karma? If, as we assume, Karma is the accumulated or acquired fate credit, either positive or negative, as the case may be, then there has to be a point at which an individual has no Karma at all. Unfortunately, we arrive at the same unanswerable point where all religious philosophy must of necessity arrive sooner or later: the condition *before* the law took effect.

Every action man takes, everything he thinks, says, does, whether on his own initiative or in response to another person's, is capable of being evaluated on merit. Some deeds or thoughts can be classified as good, others as bad, and others as indifferent. Common logic tells us this. However, from the Karmic point of view it is not enough to judge man's activities along conventional lines. Every action and reaction must also fit into the greater scheme of things; the Karmic Law asks whether the action undertaken by one individual helps or hurts another individual, and conversely, whether the activities of another individual create positive or negative factors in the receiver. First of all, Karmic Law concerns itself with impact on other individuals. Secondarily, it deals with the impact of action or thought on other elements in nature, beginning with animals and extending right through to everything in creation, whether animate or inanimate, if indeed there be such a distinction. [Recent research efforts seem to point to a needed reevaluation of our concepts of what constitutes animate in nature and what inanimate is.] In other words, a person's thoughts and actions are viewed not from *his* point of view, or even from the point of view of the one who may be the receiver of that activity, but from a very much higher reference point, as if the observer were way above the action, looking down upon it, removed from it personally, but involved in it as a scorekeeper. Although there is some evidence that specially "trained" discarnates are assigned the task of evaluating human action and enforcing the Karmic Law, justice does not rely entirely on the action of human beings, even of those who have gone into the next dimension. It appears that the law operates autonomously, in that every single action or thought by an individual registers in the "central registration office," the storehouse of universal knowledge, the Akashic records, if you wish, the focal point of administration where everything is known simultaneously and eternally, both forward and backwards in so-called time.

Karma is acquired continuously by everyone. No action is too insignificant, no thought too fleeting, nothing too small not to weigh in evidence when the balance must be restored. That moment, of course, is rebirth, a moment when retribution or reward is in order. No one can avoid creating or acquiring Karma. Karma itself is like magic: it is neither good nor bad, it depends entirely on the one creating it whether it is good or bad in the long run. A tantalizing thought presents itself as a partial explanation for the complexities of human personality. If man is the sum total of the opportunities laid out for him at the moment of birth, and is encased in a denser outer layer called the physical body, then his every action and reaction, his every thought and feeling are counted toward his next incarnation. They are, in fact, the equivalent of human personality. Or, to

110

put it more precisely, man's personality is not a monolith but a loosely constructed combination of stimuli, thoughts, feelings, actions, reactions, attitudes, and interludes, held together by the ego-consciousness, the pilot of the human personality vehicle, as it were. On this basis everything happening to one small particle of the whole may have important repercussions for the rest of the structure. This is shown in nature by the fact that individuals can be greatly influenced by comparatively small and short-lived incidents in their lives. Even major deeds need not take more than a few seconds, yet may have lasting effect for the rest of that individual's life in the particular incarnation. The amount of so-called time spent on certain actions or thoughts is quite immaterial in relationship to the impact.

Some comparatively slow developments, consuming much time, may still have only very limited meaning in terms of Karmic value. It takes only a few seconds to murder another human being, but the impact will stay with the perpetrator for the rest of his years. On the other hand, one may strive for many years to gain a certain advantage or goal, yet this effort will only weigh very slightly in the evaluation at the end of that particular individual's life. It is not even the honesty or sincerity with which one applies oneself to any given task. After all, human talents and abilities differ greatly. Then, too, we must consider that a life without previously acquired Karma is merely a theoretic assumption.

For practical purposes, and in order to understand the workings of reincarnation, we should begin with the earliest life on earth, during which some previously acquired Karma already exists. The question is, where does such Karma come from? We have no evidential information concerning the number of incarnations possible for each human being. As I have already pointed out, the evidence for transmigration or the change from

111

animal to human status is practically non-existent in scientific terms. Yet, something must have preexisted man's first incarnation as man. I have no concrete solution to offer, except the feeling that perhaps prior to a fully structured and individual personality, man may have drawn upon the forces of the environment to create Karmic preconditions. From the *second* incarnation onward, the matter is much easier to grasp. Quite obviously, the actions and thoughts of the first lifetime in a physical body as a human being will determine what happens in the next incarnation. From then on it is a matter of action and reaction, determined by a rigid sense of values which differs greatly from the conventional human set of values.

Nobody can avoid acquiring Karma, since without Karma there is no life on earth. What man can avoid, however, is to acquire *bad* Karma. Those who hold no beliefs in reincarnation will not see the need to do so, of course. It is their privilege to discover these truths at the proper time, when, unfortunately, they will be unable to correct things except by obeying and subjecting themselves to the very law they thought did not exist. But those who have learned that a system called reincarnation and Karma exists and affects them, can to some degree determine the shape of things to come in their next cycle on earth.

This does not mean that one need live a moral, strictly controlled life, dedicated to humanitarianism and denying the self. It is nearly impossible for most human beings not to acquire some negative Karma as well, even if there is a conscious effort to avoid it. We are, after all, emotional creatures, and at times allow our lower instincts to run unbridled. On balance, however, the knowing individual can leave one lifetime with a vast surplus of positive Karma and need not fear that the next incarnation will present him with too great a bill for the wrongs he has done in this one. Avoiding bad Karma requires, however,

112

that the individual be conscious of his responsibility not only to himself as an instrument of divine expression, but also towards all of his fellow men, his fellow creatures and the entire environment. The degree of responsibility towards the world in which one lives determines very largely the conditions in the next return. Unfortunately a large part of humanity is unable to grasp these very simple truths. The universe cannot function as a wholesome and harmonious creation if some elements in it persist in abusing it. It must therefore eliminate such elements by the natural means inherent in the Karmic Law.

Certain thoughts and actions are obviously negative in character, even if the individual involved is not cognizant of reincarnation evidence. To kill, to cheat, or to abuse another human being, to hurt others, to abuse animals, to steal or destroy property, all of those actions are not only morally wrong in terms of our conventional society, they are equally wrong in terms of the universal law and Karma.

But the obvious breaches of law are not the chief cause of so much Karmic debt: it is in areas that are not easily recognized as being negative that most of the negative Karma is acquired. Studied goodness, organized charity, actions designed to ease one's conscience rather than stemming from spontaneous feelings do not help one's positive Karma at all. On the other hand, actions or, as the case may be, refraining from actions that would interfere with the harmony in nature or in a fellow human being, can weigh very heavily in one's favor at the right time.

Those religions that speak of a Judgment Day are merely personalizing a continual appraisal going on under the Karmic Law. How do you avoid negative Karma? Consider yourself a vehicle of divine expression, in that you have been put on earth to perform a certain task or tasks. Do not assume that there is not a definite mission or purpose involved, for nothing in nature is accidental or wasted. By assuming that you have a job to do, determine what that job may be and once you have found it, do it as well as you are able to. In knowing what you are all about and implementing that knowledge to the best of your ability at all times you are coming closest to fulfilling the spiritual purpose of your existence. Your own inner barometer will tell you when you are on the right track or when you are off it. There is a certain feeling of satisfaction in knowing one has done something well or that one has done the right thing. Those who do not have this ability as yet within themselves, can develop it by learning to be calm and at times, introspective. Sooner or later the ability to sense what is right or wrong does come to everyone. Action taken intuitively is more likely to be correct from that point of view than logically, dissected and weighed action, influenced by the logical mind, environment and upbringing, and other external factors. *Feelings, of which intuition is part, are a direct pipeline to the reservoir of truth.*

In this connection it is not wrong to seek personal advantage or success, on any level, but it is wrong to seek it to the detriment of others. To look for fulfillment on *all* levels is not only right, but the natural and instinctive expression of a fully developed human being. To seek such progress through the destruction of other creatures, however, is wrong.

When the opportunity presents itself to advance without destroying someone in one's path, then *that* is the positive Karmic thing to do. Critics might argue that it is almost impossible to succeed in the world without stepping on or over someone else. The answer depends on the circumstances and the ways: for instance, if a clever businessman, through his own resources, acquires the capital to buy out a competitor, that competitor will have to look elsewhere for his professional fulfillment. Had he fully utilized his own resources, he would not have been bought out. The same businessman, using immoral or illegal tactics to undermine his competitor while the competitor is doing everything within his abilities to advance himself, would yield the same end result of course. The competitor would be bought out by the stronger man, but the means used to attain this end would have created negative Karma.

I am not suggesting that everyone must look out for his fellow man, in order to progress. Everyone must look out for himself, to begin with. Only when a man *consciously,* or by default, and unconsciously, causes harm or destruction to another being that negative Karma comes into effect. On the level of human life itself, through violence and war, one might argue this point of view to the extreme: how does a soldier performing his patriotic duty to defend his country and to kill an enemy compare to the murderer who kills a man for his money? Does the motivation determine the evaluation of the outcome? In my opinion, the taking of life, especially human life, is *always* negative Karma. War and violence themselves are carriers of negative Karma, consequently all actions taken as part of such activities can only lead to the acquisition of bad Karma, whether the individual concerned does so for seemingly lofty motives or not. In the words of George Bernard Shaw, "There are no just wars."

Those who advocate a completely prearranged universe devoid of all free will may argue that the selection of activities leading to bad Karma may also be predetermined for a certain individual. A Genghis Khan may have been chosen by fate to be an instrument for its own ends. Is it his fault that through his cruelties he acquires enormous amounts of negative Karma? I am not a believer in total predetermination, but feel that a degree of free will is open to all of us. It is this very important amount of decision-making that creates Karma for the next incarnation. Thus, if a Genghis Khan committed himself to the

115

role of conqueror, with all the inherent destruction and cruelties, he did so because of a sense of destiny, born from his own desires, perhaps frustrations, and not based on the inner call which alone determines a man's proper expression in each lifetime.

How do you pay off Karma? As we have seen, Karma can be either a credit or a debit, depending upon the nature of the event, situation, action or character of the individual involved. If it is a credit, then it will be paid off automatically through the intervention of the Karmic Law, and in due course. If it is a debit, it will have to be wiped out in the next life through positive actions and reactions. Contrary to the popular slogan, opposites attract, *like* attracts *like* in the esoteric world. Good Karma brings forth more good, and it seems axiomatic that the payoff for positive Karma is an increase over the previously acquired good Karma. The extent of this differs from case to case. The status quo is not in keeping with the universal aspect of life: everything moves at all times. Positive Karma will not be paid off by negative Karma in a subsequent incarnation. But positive results in one lifetime must be based upon corresponding positive factors in the previous one or previous ones. *In other words, everything must be earned.* An individual may or may not accept the Karmic payoff in good grace, but he cannot prevent the discharge of Karma from one incarnation to the next. The idea that someone may refuse to accept the good is not as far-fetched as it may sound: some individuals, out of extreme modesty, or more likely out of a psychological fear that they cannot properly reciprocate, are in the habit of rejecting good things coming to them. With Karma, there is no choice. There cannot be any choice since the law operates naturally, impersonally, directly, without the intermediary of a human element. Even if an individual wanted to reject the blessings stemming from previous positive Karma, whom would

116

he address his complaint to? Not the deity, since the deity creates the Law but does not administer it. Not the "Board of Directors" as I like to call them, those advanced souls who have been entrusted with the supervision of an orderly progression from one lifetime to another. They have charge of operating the Karmic Law, but they do not have the right to suspend it.

Advanced individuals who understand this law can build from one incarnation to the next until they reach the highest levels, at which point they may elect to become members of the elite of beings, sometimes called the Masters. To be sure, one does not accumulate good Karma deliberately, in a coldblooded, cunning or planned fashion. Rather, one accumulates it by being in tune with the spirit of the universe, by *training oneself to react* instantly and intuitively in the right way, no matter what the challenge or situation may be.

Thus, the matter of acquiring further positive Karma is not one of logic but one of feeling. Feeling, in turn, cannot be acquired at will the way one acquires a bank account. It is a delicate expression of soul which results when the trinity of mind, body, and spirit are in harmony, exercising a maximum of interaction, and utilizing in full the force inherent in it from the moment of its creation. In popular terms, knowing oneself, understanding one's potentials, strengths and weaknesses, and accepting oneself with all the faults that may be present, at the same time placing oneself at the disposal of the forces of fate, realizing that one is but a small particle of a large and unified system and being alive in the fullest sense of the word—those are the sure methods by which one increases positive Karma.

If one has done something in one lifetime that must be classed as negative Karma, it will have to be paid off in some fashion in the next life. Occasionally, it may take several life-times to be fully paid off, or the neglect, the negative factor, stemming from one incarnation may only be paid off several incarnations later. Every case is individual and different, but one thing is sure: bad Karma must be paid off *eventually.* This is how it works. If an action has been committed in one lifetime that comes under the classification of negative Karma, the same situation will not recur in the following lifetime or in one of the next incarnations. Rather, parallel situations will be "thrown into the path" of the individual, to be acted upon by that individual as his free will dictates. Since the situations are only similar in terms of merit, but not in terms of circumstances, the individual being tested cannot anticipate them or connect them with happenings in an earlier lifetime. He is, therefore, solely dependent upon his own resources, his good or bad judgment, as the case may be.

The only exception to this rule are the comparatively few cases where reincarnation memories, or rather small traces of them, have been permitted to remain. I have found that this is the case only when a lifetime has been cut short, or when some major situation in one lifetime has not come to fruition. Thus, such reincarnation memories seem to be in the nature of bonus arrangements, giving the individual a small head start in the next incarnation, by allowing him some insight as to his previous doings. In this way, he may benefit from the information and apply the knowledge when parallel occurrences happen to him, if he is alert to the deeper meaning of the event, of course. Only those conversant with reincarnation theory can properly evaluate such links.

For instance, let us assume that an individual has made gains in his business by dealing dishonestly with a friend. In his next lifetime a situation may come his way in which he has the opportunity of dealing again with a friend in some totally different business matter. Sooner or later he will be put before a decision, whether or not to take advantage of his friend. If he follows his natural instincts, without also listening to the inner

118

voice of harmony, he may simply do the obvious thing and take advantage of his friend. But if he is attuned to the deeper meanings of such challenges, he may reject the opportunity and come to his friend's aid, instead of taking advantage of a faltering business by buying it out, lend his friend support so that he may go on with new strength. That would be discharging negative Karma. It would not gain him additional good Karma in the following incarnation, but he would have no negative Karma to shoulder either. The balance would have been restored.

Everything in the universe must be in balance, and that which is not, must swing back and forth until its movement brings it to a point where total harmony reigns again. For when the forces of plus and minus are equal, they join each other and create a new whole, which is neither positive nor negative but contains elements of both. Polarity is that which separates, but it also creates the driving force to purify and eventually come together again. When full harmony is reached, polarity serves to keep the balance.

A particularly sensitive point in reincarnation research concerns illness in individuals, when there is no apparent reason for such illness to exist. *Can illnesses be Karmically caused?* As I have explained in *Beyond Medicine,* my recent book on psychical healing, most illnesses are caused by a state of imbalance in the etheric body of the individual. Only accidents or diseases clearly due to neglect should be attributed to physical causes. But some, if not all, of these illnesses and accidents may be due to a Karmic debt. In cases where an individual has physically hurt another, causing that person to be ill or crippled, the individual himself becomes similarly afflicted in the next incarnation. His suffering wipes out the suffering of the one he has mistreated. This need not be the identical illness or affliction, but maybe in a different part of the body; nevertheless, in its impact it would parallel the situation suffered by the other person in the previous incarnation. Do we then inherit the illness and afflictions of our previous sojourn on earth? On the surface, it would seem unfair for us to be responsible in this lifetime for something committed by our previous self, living a totally different life, and being an entirely different person. Such responsibility and inherited doom smacks of the idea of original sin propounded by the Roman Catholic Church and rejected, quite rightly, by the majority of progressive thinkers. But it is nothing of the sort. In being given a chance to make up for a wrong done by us in a previous life, even if it means suffering in this one, we are in the end ennobling our own soul, helping it to progress by eliminating the negative aspects from the past. If an illness or affliction has been recognized as Karmic, it does not follow that we cannot do something about it. We can deal with it as if it were an illness caused by wrongful thinking or an imbalance in our own system. The techniques in dealing with it are exactly the same, and as a result we may eliminate or overcome the Karmically caused illness. By doing so we are not setting Karma aside. The incidence of the illness of affliction itself is the Karmic debt being offered for *payment:* our *efforts* expanded on our own behalf to eliminate the illness or affliction is a proper positive response under the Karmic Law. By doing the "right" thing about our illness, we would be acquiring positive Karma, were it not for the fact that we are extinguishing an old negative Karma. Thus the slate is clean; there is neither loss nor gain.

Karmic Law operates through parallel situations, carefully evaluating conditions in such a way that we are not given any hints that there may be a connection between what is happening to us now and what has happened to us before. Since the majority of people do not have reincarnation memories in the waking condition, and only a fraction remembers sufficiently in the dream state to be able to draw conclusions from their reincarnation flashes, we can only guess that some event in a past life may be responsible for our present predicament.

But one life must be lived at a time: decisions and reactions must be based upon our personal feelings, regardless of how many lives we may have lived before. The Karmic Law would be meaningless if we knew that we were being tested or that some events in our lives were due to a similar event in another lifetime. Likewise, the Karmic Law would be without sense if we did not have free will in deciding, if only intuitively, what to do about each and every situation we are faced with. Man's free will is the very foundation of his kinship with the Deity: if he was created in His image, as the religionists claim, then it would seem a cruel persiflage if man could not determine his reactions when faced with the forces of destiny.

But bad Karma to be worked off or good Karma to be increased are by no means the only reference points from incarnation to incarnation. When there are traces of previous memories, they are in many cases due to *unfinished business.* Unfinished business may concern itself with a mission in one life which was cut short by tragic circumstances and could not be accomplished. It may have to do with setting things right in some way, or it may refer to the carrying out of a trust.

We know that a large portion of authentic apparitions is due to unfinished business, compelling the entity to seek recognition in order to make itself heard or felt. This compulsion is strong enough to carry it from the next dimension back into the present one and until the unfinished business has been disposed of the compulsion to reappear will continue. Similarly, unfinished business in one incarnation may carry with it enough compulsion to emerge again at some stage in the next one. In some cases, this manifests itself when the individual is only a child, while with others it begins to emerge after the teenage years. Since unfinished business can range almost the entire width of human experiences, it is difficult to pinpoint the tell-tale marks of such causative factors. But there is present an overriding compulsion, a driving force to do certain things, to be in certain places, to seek out certain individuals or situations, which cannot be explained on the basis of the current incarnation. As a matter of fact, in many instances it goes counter to present inclinations. People of one type of background will seek out people of an entirely different background, and feel completely comfortable with them, while feeling out of place with their own. This applies to places and occupations as well. Even skills acquired in one incarnation may be remembered, gradually or suddenly, in the next one, if they were in some way not fully utilized in the earlier lifetime. This accounts for a number of amazing situations where individuals seemingly possess talents, interests, and inclinations for which there is no rational basis in their present circumstances.

But unfinished business may also pertain to personal matters; it may create difficult problems in one's emotional life, it may even create social and legal difficulties. Of this further on in this book. How does one dispose of unfinished business? First, it is important to recognize it and to put it into the right perspective in relation to the present circumstances. Can one deal with unfinished business under the current circumstances, taking into account one's abilities, powers, environment, and obligations? If there does not seem to be any insurmountable barrier against it, the wisest thing would be to attempt to pick up where a previous lifetime has left off. The more one realizes the nature of the unfinished business, partially through snatches of reincarnation memories, partially perhaps by observing one's peculiar inclinations and unconscious activities, the more can one gradually put oneself into the shoes of the person whose business was left unfinished earlier. Using intuition as much as possible, circumstances will present themselves which demand certain reactions. If the synthesis between present personality and the remnants of the previous one is a good one, instinctive moves will be made and the unfinished business brought to a conclusion. It may not always be the identical business, to be sure; parallels are also common under these circumstances.

Either way, the matter is taken out of the Karmic relationship and one is able to move forward in the present incarnation. Ignoring unfinished business when one has become aware of it is not advisable. To begin with, it won't go away. One cannot simply suppress it or look the other way, because the more one tries to avoid it the more it is likely to establish itself in both conscious and unconscious minds. The advice of professional psychics in such matters is also of doubtful value; unless the psychic involved is of superior quality such readings tend to reflect too much guesswork, generalities, prestoral advice and otherwise useless material. Far better sources of information lie buried within oneself, if one learns to tap such sources through meditation, periods of withdrawal from the world, and a progressive, steady technique of listening to the Inner Voice, which we all have.

Unfinished business is not due to an accident or neglect of nature. Nature does not err. But there are individual cases where proper application of the universal law demands an interruption of the business at hand, even though on the surface of it this seems unreasonable. If, as I assume, all data pertaining to an individual are fed into a kind of computer, although a spiritual one, and if this spiritual computer comes up with certain negative suggestions based on the sum total of what was fed into it, the smooth continuance of that individual's mission on the earth plane in this particular incarnation must be disturbed in order to satisfy *previously* acquired Karma. Even the way in which we are born and in which we die is a Karmic matter, determined by, and dependent upon previous conditions and reactions. Theoretically, at least, only the "young soul," the soul just created by the "system" is relatively free from such burdens, since it comes into the cycle of life without previous testing. But even the new soul brings into its first encounter with life certain environmental factors acquired at the very moment of birth.

Very common occurrences involving Karma, both negative and positive, are the links between millions of people who do not know each other in the present incarnation. Almost everybody has met someone at one time or another and experienced the distinct impression that they have known each other before, yet are unable to determine when and where their relationships began. Sometimes this recognition is sudden and dramatic. Some of these experiences are classed under the déjà vu phenomenon, because they give the feeling of "haven't I met you some place before?" People meet for the first time and are able to describe each other's whims and likes instantly and without previous knowledge. People can sometimes remember having been together in strange places and under strange circumstances, yet, in the cold light of their present lives, there is no rational basis for their assumptions. This phenomenon is so widespread, so common, that it appears to me to be one of the prime elements in the reincarnation system. *Links* between people are important, but perhaps even more important is the *recognition* of such links. Undoubtedly the majority of these links are simply overlooked, shrugged off as coincidences, strange occurrences without particular meaning, or deliberately ignored.

I maintain that two people never meet without some significant purpose being involved. This purpose may only come to fruition *after* the initial meeting or perhaps at a much later time; but two entities in this universe do not meet up with each other unless a third purpose is involved and meant to be dealt with. The difficulty lies in recognizing first, that there is a link between them, and second, what the purpose of their meeting is in terms of universal or Karmic Law. Those who have undergone some esoteric training will perhaps be able to recognize some of the meaning inherent in such meetings. But people who still cling to the materialistic concept of coincidence and accident in nature, are not likely to see the deeper meanings behind such so-called "chance meetings."

I will discuss the difficulties sometimes arising from such chance meetings in a later chapter, but links of this kind are of the utmost importance not only in accomplishing one's mission in life, but also in furthering the other person's purpose. The more we understand the meaning and the meaningfulness of links between people, the more we begin to understand the meaning of the reincarnation system.

Sometimes, the pursuit of links can be exaggerated. People who are firm believers in reincarnation may see deep significance in everyone they meet, everyone in their family and among their friends, to the point where the entire notion becomes grossly exaggerated. Mistakenly, they will attempt to identify everyone they know as having been a close friend or relation in a previous lifetime or perhaps several lifetimes ago. Thus, the present mother becomes a daughter in another life, the rejected lover is the successful rival in the last incarnation, the child which reminds one so much of one's grandmother, is the grandmother reincarnated, and so forth. Return of a loved one or a friend between one incarnation and the next one is possible, of course, but recognition of such relationships must be based on *evidential factors:* certainly, the life readings being dispensed by self-appointed experts for a certain sum of money do not offer such meticulous proof. There is no need to disregard scientific standards in this field, where such standards are the only safeguard against delusion, whether perpetrated by others or by self.

125

If you meet someone and become convinced that you've lived before in the same place and at the same time, you must search for details of that life together which are capable of being checked out objectively in the files and records of various libraries and research societies. If the life together was in some distant civilization of which there are no research records, such as Atlantis or Lemuria, the matter of proof becomes very difficult, of course. But whenever you are dealing with a known civilization and time in human history, proof of existence of certain individuals can be had in the majority of cases. Even if the individuals concerned were of minor status and thus not likely to be found in historical records, indirect evidence can be obtained through the knowledge of circumstances, ways of life, terms used for certain articles or conditions, and, in general, by carefully observing knowledge not otherwise explicable in terms of the individual's present circumstances and background.

The question still remains: who decreed the Law of Karma, and who administers it? If we are to believe that God is contained in all of us and that we are part of God, then it would appear that the Karmic Law was also in some way and in some measure created by us, the living universe, in order to have a set of rules to keep this universe in harmony and balance. It appears to administer itself by the very virtue of its infallability; its omniscience makes it possible for The Law to be aware of all that occurs everywhere, forever, and thus, quasi-automatically, take the necessary steps to create the conditions that are likely to balance the system for specific individuals.

It may be a little like a Calder mobile, in which the delicate construction can be put into motion by a very slight touch. Eventually it returns to its properly balanced condition. The waves, that is to say the movements the mobile makes while adjusting itself and returning to its state of perfect balance, may be compared to the encounters between human beings and situations with which they must cope one way or another. What

126

remains unanswered, of course, is the age-old question; who started it all and what is he doing now, if in fact he is a he and not a she or an it? This is not the place to give you an answer to that question, but by exploring with scientific detachment and at the same time an open mind the results of the Law of Karma, we may come a giant step closer to the understanding of the nature of the system in which the Karmic Law is an important element.

Chapter 9
Soul Mates

When we are dealing with destiny and how it effects the social and moral order of our times, we inevitably come into conflict with some aspects of these man-made orders. That is not surprising since the social and moral order of each period is not the result of any divine inspiration, of any spiritual unfoldment from within, but usually the result of economic pressures, religious fears and prejudices, and other negative factors not truly in tune with the natural development and expression of man. The social and moral order in which we live may be progressive in some aspects, especially technology, but it is essentially still the old order of things, and the old order never changeth.

There is an overriding desire on the part of those who live in this old structure to put everything in its proper place. Whenever some element, be it an idea, a human being, or a power source, gets out of line, it causes waves which the majority likes to avoid. This desire to put everything in its proper place can grow to grotesque heights. It may be understandable when we are dealing with monogamy; the commandment against adultery. It may be understandable when the priest or minister of a specific religion insists that the worshipper adhere to his religion only, to the exclusion of all others. It becomes less acceptable in the professional life of a man, when the specialist is worshipped as the hero of the day while the Renaissance man becomes more and more suspect. Anyone who has knowledge in several fields is not likely to have an easy professional life. The age of the specialist is upon us, and going against this concept is by and large resented by those who are unable to broaden their horizons sufficiently to take in more than one form of endeavor. In this specialization lies the germ of destruction: it may well be that a specialist wanted at a certain time or juncture of events is absent, and there is no one to take his place. Under such circumstances, technology may rapidly disintegrate, as many philosophers have already predicted.

In this rigid social and moral order there is still very little tolerance for the aberration. Monogamy is still the rule, although a rapid succession of marriages is not considered sinful or illegal. With the coming of the age of explicitness, sex has become a commonplace expression. The older and more affluent generation accepts it placidly, trying to cover up its traces as much as possible and pretending that nothing special is happening. The younger, more honest generation needs no such camouflage: at last, they have come to grips with the honesty of sexual expression and in so doing have gotten closer to the natural way of life than any generation before them within the memory of mankind.

But as yet there is no question that relationships based upon previous lifetimes cannot seriously be considered as bases for close relationships in this life. While the interest in parapsychology and the occult sciences has risen in recent years and reached a kind of plateau of respectability even among the broad masses, this interest has still the aura of curiosity about it. Only a comparatively small segment of the world population truly understands the deeper meaning of living life on the esoteric level.

The theory behind the existence of soul mates goes back to the earliest history of mankind. Even in the Stone Age religion called, appropriately, "The Old Religion," one of the prime motivations of leading a good and useful life was to be reborn again near the loved one and find the loved one again in the next incarnation. In medieval times, the idea of the divinely joined couple runs through many romantic narratives. The German poet Johann Wolfgang Goethe wrote a novel called *Die Wahlverwandtschaften,* meaning "elective affinities," relationships by choice. It was his contention that every human being had a perfect mate (of the opposite sex) waiting to be discovered. Goethe expressed in poetic form a philosophy which is probably the deepest and most significant element of all esoteric teachings.

At the beginning, it is thought, the soul was created as an exterior expression of the Godhead, a unit unto itself and therefore neither male nor female, but both. Sometime in great antiquity the soul was split into a male and a female half and sent forth into the world to prove itself. Through testing and purification, the two halves were forever striving to reunite again. In the process, the dynamics of the world were achieved. As a new result, a vastly strengthened and purified double soul would emerge, to become, perhaps, what the philosopher Nietzsche called Superman.

Since the soul mates were originally part of a larger unit, they would be possessed of knowledge that need not be explained from one to the other. Consequently, one of the earmarks of finding the true soul mate was immediate recognition, instant understanding and communication beyond logical explanation, even beyond telepathy, accompanied by deep feelings of mutual love. The longing of one soul mate for the other is, in the eyes

131

of the esoteric, the major driving force that makes man search the universe for fulfillment. Only by reaching out to this ideal soul mate can he hope to accomplish his destiny. It does not follow that everyone of us finds the soul mate destined for him or her, but the act of reaching toward it is the important thing. By that very longing, the dynamic force of motivated desire is set into motion, and the multitude of such desires creates the power reservoir whence creative people obtain their inspirations and driving force.

Soul mates are not only physically attuned to each other, and consequently perfect for each other in the sexual sense, but they share mutual interests, have identical outlooks on all phases of life, and are in every respect compatible one to the other. Soul mates are not necessarily ideal mates in terms of contemporary standards; they may differ greatly in age, social or economic background, or even race. As a matter of fact, some soul mates may be so radically different in outer appearance that the proof of their relationship lies in overcoming their differences rather than in accentuating them. But soul mates are always one male and one female, for there is neither reference to nor tolerance of homosexuality in esoteric philosophy. This is understandable since a plus and minus attract each other while two pluses or two minuses accomplish the opposite.

But soul mates are by no means one of a kind. Everyone of us has several potential soul mates, though he may never meet up with any of them. From the material I have investigated, and the philosophies I am familiar with, it would appear that each case is different and each personality requires a different set of circumstances and number of soul mates to find his whole self again. Some individuals may do so with one perfect soul mate. Some people will find such a soul mate and actually marry them. The majority rarely do, but those who are esoterically awake, will continue to hope that someday they will meet their soul mates, even though they may be married to someone else

132

at the time. This, of course, creates another set of problems. If they find their perfect soul mates, should they abandon their conventional mate? If they do, they may find happiness but society may condemn them. If they do not, they will live with a sense of frustration to the end of their physical days.

Those who have the potential of uniting with several soul mates in their lives, usually the leaders of this world, the creative people, those who have much to give to the world, find one or several of these potential soul mates as they move through the years. For them to deny themselves the opportunity to unite with them, if only for a limited period of time, would cut off the free flow of the very energies they need to continue their mission on earth.

One has to be sure that the member of the opposite sex one has met is truly a soul mate, and that physical desires do not create a mirage. Many are the tests by which a true soul mate is recognized. Above all, comparison of previously held knowledge about a number of subjects, possibly the question of whether both soul mates felt identical reactions toward each other at the same time, and possible reincarnation memories, should all be taken into consideration before a conclusion is reached. On the other hand, conventional social, moral and religious considerations should be carefully avoided in judging such a relationship. Frequently, the very point of such an unusual relationship is that it must be *outside* convention. In overcoming one's fears of conventionality, one earns the right to unite with the other soul mate. If it is a question of a number of soul mates during a lifetime, both partners should realize that the union may be of a limited duration for a purpose: once that which was meant to be accomplished by their coming together again has been completed, they must each go their separate ways to unite with other respective soul mates to accomplish still other purposes meant for them as a means of fulfilling their destiny.

At times, a couple becomes involved one with the other

without realizing that they are actually soul mates. In the course of time, they discover that their relationship was not merely a physical or spiritual or emotional one, but develops beyond the usual elements into a deeper relationship and one day they discover that they were soul mates and stem from a common source. In such cases, of course, it may well be that the couple stays together to the end of their earthly lives, no longer seeking other soul mates. In realizing that each individual may have more than one perfect soul mate to merge with we should not understand this necessarily as an invitation to a kind of esoteric polygamy, but merely one of possibilities. The fact that a number of potentially equal soul mates or combinations of soul mates are in existence may also mean that a particular individual has more than one chance to merge with a perfect partner, under different circumstances, but with equal results. This is particularly important in cases where an unhappy love affair creates the false impression in one partner that his life's purpose has been aborted and that he will never find the same kind of love again. Remember, we are *all* unique, and at the same time, *nothing* in the universe is unique. The uniqueness of self is repeated in myriads of wondrous ways throughout the universe, equal, parallel, similar and yet not quite the same.

Let us assume that two people meet, both of them not free in the conventional sense, and that they discover a deep longing for each other, far beyond physical or emotional desire. If they are esoterically inclinded, they may discover that they are soul mates. To become one, a perfect union on all levels, physical, mental, and spiritual, is not a question of indulging themselves. The joy of such unions lies not in recognizing their previous relationship, but in implementing the opportunity which so patently has come their way for a reason. They cannot afford to overlook the opportunity, to offend fate. They do not only have the chance to unite again as they were once united, they

134

have the sacred duty to do so in order to recharge their energies for further accomplishments in tune with the *Patterns of Destiny*. Avoiding such relationships leads to individual unhappiness and will surely cause the two potential soul mates to slow their progress. Furthermore, they will each and individually face a parallel situation again at some time in the future, whether in the same incarnation or in the next one, and will again be tested as to their responsibilities and the maturity of their decisions. It is therefore inescapable that when such conditions are recognized as cases of soul mates, direct and positive action is taken by both partners to fulfill the manifest desire of destiny.

Chapter 10
Probing the True Self

There are three tasks that lie ahead of everyone who wishes to get the full benefit of reincarnation knowledge. First, how to expand consciousness; second, how to fulfill your life's purpose, and third, how to find out, if possible, who you were in a previous life. These three questions are basic inquiries into what you, the individual, are all about: but they are also basic questions concerning the system under which all of us operate.

How to expand consciousness? Certainly, a fair amount of reading, especially books of substance, will help prepare the way for a better understanding of self. In addition, discussion with like-minded individuals may bring out further points of importance. But, essentially, expanding consciousness is a lonely effort which will succeed only if the individual puts his best foot forward, so to speak. Belief, conviction that the system exists and that one is part of it, are valuable but not required as a precondition for success or even understanding. The conviction that there is a system other than the material one and that one is able to expand consciousness are very helpful in making it work better and sooner. But even the skeptic, even the negative person, may proceed along the suggested lines and succeed eventually, whether he expects to or not. Consciousness means to be aware of self and the environment, to be cognizant of what was before and what may lay ahead, and to have an understanding, both intuitively and logically, of the purpose of life in all its components. Anything less than that represents but partial consciousness.

The majority of human beings are only dimly aware of the full range of their potential or of the deeper meanings of their existence. Thus, the first step towards full consciousness is to examine the component parts of self. Then one realizes that there is a trinity of body, mind, and spirit in operation and that the trinity must work together at all times, in harmony and union, in order to produce results. Keeping this "machinery" in excellent condition is therefore a must. Expanding consciousness, strange as it may seem, will depend also on the physical condition of the body, the proper upkeep of what philosophers have called the "temple of the deity," exercises, especially the kind taught in yoga, proper breathing, proper sleeping and eating habits, and many other aspects of physical well-being. Consciousness does not expand in a sick body. True, there are extreme cases where a crippled or otherwise afflicted individual may overcome the limitations of his physical self and expand his spiritual and mental horizons far beyond that which might be expected of him. But those are cases of overcoming difficulties as part of Karmic efforts and not the norm. Mental consciousness can be expanded through learning, through an unsatiable curiosity, taking a leaf from Albert Schweitzer's interest in all living things, exploring the universe and informing oneself in every way about the world in which we live. I don't mean to catalog the universe in its components, but to grasp the deeper relationships between individual parts of the universe, how it works and how it came about, if one is able to consider such questions. Look behind things, rather than skimming over them!

Perhaps the most difficult aspect to expand is spiritual consciousness. To begin with, it is somewhat difficult to define. Perhaps the best way to describe it is as the awareness of a higher order of things, the understanding that one is only a small particle of a major system in which there is a supreme power, even though one does not quite understand what this power is or why it is there. In addition, it means being responsible and responsive to the needs of all existing entities, living or seemingly inorganic nature around oneself, in that one sees or feels part of the deity in *all* of it.

Perhaps Albert Schweitzer, in expressing his belief in the "sanctity in all life," approached it more accurately than any other recent contemporary. Spiritual consciousness, once accepted as a way of life, will never permit one to return to a materialistic point of view. The enlightenment stays, whether or not the individual has a successful life in the material sphere. Spiritual consciousness does not mean that one need be a medium or receiver of communications from the world of spirit, although many of those who have accepted it and developed their consciousness in that respect have eventually found themselves to be highly sensitive to the vibrations from that finer world. But the more one partakes of spiritual consciousness, the more sensitive the personality becomes, and communication is a natural result of this development.

The expansion of spiritual consciousness is encouraged by keen observation of the things happening to oneself, the people one meets, the opportunities and events one encounters and what their deeper meanings might be. Regular meditation sessions can be of invaluable help. They need not be rigid in terms of concentrating upon a particular image, such as some Indian teachers insist upon. Merely the act of opening oneself up to the Inner Voice is sufficient, provided these sessions are undertaken in regular patterns, thus establishing a rhythm in time. This is very important, for haphazard meditation does not really do

139

very much. But if one has established a rhythmic pattern of regularly scheduled meditation sessions, even if they are only five or ten minutes at a time, it must not be interrupted; for even one breach in the rhythmical pattern will reduce the individual to the point of departure and the effort will have to be made again.

During these sessions it may happen that exterior forces manifest, or that the voices of the deceased are heard. This need not frighten the individual in any way, since it is a natural development and part of expanding one's consciousness.

Another technique which may be helpful in developing a wider consciousness, is experimenting with psychometry. Psychometry is the simplest form of ESP. It consists of touching an object and deriving certain information from it about its owner or former owner. In psychometry we assume that the object is coated with a fine film of electromagnetic particles containing the essence of the owner's image. Bits and pieces of information are thus retained in this film and may be reconstructed and read by anyone touching the object at a later date. By doing so, we are able to "tune in" not only on events in the distant past, but also in distant places. Knowledge not ordinarily available to the experimenter becomes part of his consciousness and he is able to "read" the object, and with it, the owner. By experimenting with such ESP abilities, we sharpen our consciousness and make it more readily accessible to the search for reincarnation memories of our own, which is our goal.

How to fulfill your life's purpose? Expanding consciousness on all three levels, physical, mental, and spiritual and making constant use of these faculties in your daily life will inevitably lead to a fuller understanding of your purpose in this cycle on earth. *It is important to realize that nothing can prevent an individual from attaining his goal once that goal is fully realized in his own consciousness.* Those who falter or fail are individuals who do not fully understand their purpose or the ways in which their consciousness should be employed. I make no exception from this statement, daring though it may appear to some. It is my contention that a conviction of being able to accomplish certain ends would not have been imbedded in a person's consciousness, unless it were also possible to attain such a goal, conditions being right. I have little belief in wishful thinking and immature fantasy as explanation for a man's sincere and convinced drive towards a certain goal, just because the goal seems at times out of line with the reality of the person's environment or status.

When your strongest desire towards accomplishment of one kind or another is met with actual realization, you will know that the deep sense of satisfaction accompanying this realization is more than the feeling of a successful individual: It is the awareness that one has done that which fate has expected of one, one has lived up to the expectation not only in terms of material fulfillment but also in the sense that one has had to overcome many difficulties. Mostly, these obstacles were overcome because of the deep conviction that they *could* be overcome, and that one had to accomplish that which one's Inner Voice dictated. In other words, unswerving belief in oneself and the mission one has embarked upon were based on a sense of destiny. Not only do they yield positive results, but upon completion the deep sense of fulfillment, which at times resembles a joyful closeness to the deity itself.

An unused talent, an ability going to waste because the individual lacks confidence, or because the individual feels no sense of responsibility toward nature for having given him this talent, represents the other side of the coin: Nature does not waste her resources. Every talent, every ability handed out to individuals is given for a reason: The talent or ability must be

141

used to the hilt. We do not have the choice of accepting or rejecting our talents. If we refuse to accept the responsibility that comes with a given ability, we are in fact committing a kind of sin of ommission. The very fact that we are aware of certain abilities requires us to use them, and use them fully. Anything less than our best effort is equally objectionable from the wider point of view of the universal law. This does not run counter to free will: We still have complete free will in coping with given situations or conditions when they occur in our lives. We are not told in precise terms how to use our talents or abilities, merely to use them well. There are many ways in which a given talent can benefit mankind, nature, and the individual as well. The way and the method are part of our free will.

A gifted singer may pursue a career in opera, the commercial theater, motion pictures, the concert stage, or perhaps only sing for free to the sick and the poor. All of these conditions would fulfill the initial premise that the talent be used in constructive ways. A man handy at building things need not become a construction engineer. He may be a city planner, a contractor, a designer of buildings, or he may be a foreman, or perhaps only the man who fixes the house of his neighbors when the neighbor can't do it himself. In all of these cases the ability is put to good use. The range of the effectiveness of that ability is of no importance. What I am pointing out is that there is no compulsion to use a talent to ultimate worldly success; quite to the contrary. Success can be measured in many other terms. What is unforgivable and unacceptable in terms of the universal law is the neglect or the denegation of a given talent.

A number of people may seemingly not have any special talents or abilities. They may merely serve as "links" between others. The purpose of a link is to allow destiny to connect individual number one with individual number two.

142

Since nothing may be done by fate contrary to natural law, the Karmic Law sometimes requires maneuvering and long-term planning so that the purpose of the law may be fulfilled without perverting or circumventing the natural sequence of events. One of the prime factors in such maneuvering is the link, even the chain of links, whereby the purpose of bringing certain individuals together is fulfilled through the intermediary of one or several others. These links have by themselves nothing to do with the two individuals being brought together. But by being there they make the connection possible and are therefore just as important as the ultimate principals. It would appear that a majority of individuals are indeed links rather than principals with specific talents or special abilities.

Anticipating when one becomes a link is of course impossible. Consequently, a general sense of willingness and availability should one be selected as a link will be all that is required of an individual, in order to obey the Karmic Law. From the principal's point of view, that is the individual who may be approached by either another principal or a link leading to another principal, it should be remembered that opportunities are frequently disguised in order to test the individual's free will, in order to see what decision he or she may make. I have found it wisest to accept any opportunity, any occasion, almost any invitation to meet others, for one never knows what will be the result. One may not meet anyone of significance, but one may meet someone who will be a link to another situation and it is that second or third or fourth situation where the purpose lies. Nature has a sure way of bringing people together it wants to bring together, but it sometimes takes the long way around to do it. If you want to be sure you do not miss an opportunity to advance yourself on the ladder of progress, examine everything coming your way, from invitations to opportunities to meetings with strangers to suggestions about travel to books, magazines and newspapers coming your way—anything and everything for possible leads, links, and hints that may prove beneficial to your advancement. Never assume that these things are without meaning, accidental or coincidental. You may not always succeed in discovering the purpose of such events, or clues, and frequently the purpose may be very minor, but you should always try to examine such happenings for hidden motives, deeper meanings or links. Only then can you be sure that you are doing your best in cooperating with the forces of destiny towards the full and successful realization of your potentials.

Chapter 11
How to Find Out Who You Were

Perhaps I should begin by telling my readers how *not* to go about it. Far too many otherwise critical and sensible people fall victim to false "life readers," who promise them detailed and far-reaching accounts of all of their previous lives, going back to the very dawn of history. These so-called life readings often contain quasi-historical data which no one can check. The names given for individuals allegedly identical with the present incumbent are frequently not even linguistically correct. This is not surprising, since the majority of the so-called life readings are done by people with very little educational background. Those who sell such misinformation at anything from fifty dollars to a $150 per person are perhaps not entirely motivated by gain. In some cases, at least, they may sincerely believe that their musings, or induced fantasies have validity. Eventually they convince themselves that they are right. In some instances, individuals impressed with the accomplishments of Edgar Cayce feel they can emulate the great prophet. Others go into self-induced semitrances, during which they feel their spirit controls or discarnate friends supply the information required for their business of giving life readings for a fee. It is entirely possible that some of this material does indeed come from discarnate sources. This does not make it any more correct. We must always keep in mind that passing across the boundary between physical and spiritual life does in no way bring instant wisdom or nobility. *There are on the Other Side a large number of individuals who have learned absolutely nothing by dying, and who have therefore no additional knowledge to offer.* If such entities communicate with the purveyor of life readings, it is very likely that the information is just as concocted as if it were only the work of the flesh-and-blood person.

This does in no way indicate that genuine life readings cannot be had also. But the earmark of the authentic material is authenticity of detail, at least some evidence that names, places and dates can be checked out in historical records, and, even more important that the individual for whom the reading is done, recognizes some of the environments or situations suggested by the life reader as coinciding or paralleling his or her own impressions and feelings *prior* to seeking the life reading.

Favorites among would-be life readers are such exotic countries as Egypt, Babylonia, Tibet, and the East in general; ancient Greece is also very popular as is the time of the crucifiction and the environment around Jesus. Such unglamorous places as Bulgaria or Switzerland, for instance, or periods in history when nothing of great impact transpired, rarely show up in the professional life readings provided by these individuals. To do a genuine life reading for a person without being in the presence of that person is extremely difficult, if not impossible. Some life-reading material may be deduced from psychometric touches, if an object is submitted for analysis, but even that does not lend itself to a truly detailed life reading. It must be remembered that the average person seeking a commercial life reading sends his name and address, possibly his astrological sign, and requests the reading. Some eager beavers may even include details about themselves which makes the task of the false life reader that much easier. He can then invent a particularly pleasing past life in retrospect, making very sure that the earlier incarnations were much nicer than the present one.

How then does one proceed to get a *real* life reading? First of all, there is a tremendous amount of material contained in the Edgar Cayce records at Virginia Beach, Virginia. People interested in their own past may contact the Association for Research and Enlightenment in Virginia Beach and inquire whether their names happen to be listed in the life readings given by the late Edgar Cayce. Cayce based his interpretations on the Akashic records, which were apparently open to him during the trance state. There are undoubtedly some authentic life readers, especially in India and the Far East, who can reach the same sources as Cayce did, also in the trance state. But the average individual, especially those living in the United States and Europe, do not have easy access to such individuals. Especially if the interested party lives in a small town, far from the metropolitan centers where competent psychics are generally found, the matter becomes one of great difficulty.

There are two avenues open to delve into the question of previous incarnations. First, in consulting professional mediums with good reputations, and in sitting with such mediums time and again, material pertaining to the sitter's past may eventually come through one of the communicators. It should not be initiated, no questions should be asked, for developments of this kind must be spontaneous and unsought. The chance that something of this type will eventually be said is about 50 percent, especially if the sittings continue for a considerable period of time. Psychics who deal with communications from discarnates or in personal readings pertaining to the present and future of individuals are probably best equipped to receive material from the individual's past incarnations as well, provided this information stems from external sources who use the medium merely as channels of communication. If the individual has not had any inkling of a previous life prior to the sitting, that is to say, no overt knowledge of having been incarnated before, it will be up to the communicators and their judgment whether some information about previous lives should be given. There are cases where this may be considered advantageous, and there are others where it may not be. Under no circumstances can one wrest such information from the discarnate communicators, since they too must obey the universal law, including the Karmic Law. Disclosure of details from previous lives may seriously interfere with the judgment of the individual concerned in the present incarnation.

On the other hand there are methods which do not require recourse to a medium at all, whether professional or amateur. The individual himself can, under certain circumstances, draw upon the storehouse of knowledge within himself to determine what previous lives have already occurred in his consciousness. Assuming that the individual is not one of those very few who are new souls, that is to say, do not have a previous incarnation to fall back upon, but had one or more incarnations prior to the present one, the questioner should first of all set aside specific times of the day for meditation periods devoted entirely to the question of reincarnation. These moments should be at a time of day when his physical body is considerably more tired than in the midst of activities. During such states of physical tiredness, even mental tiredness, the bonds between conscious and unconscious minds are considerably lessened and psychic material is more likely to rise to the surface. The room should be remote from human activities, particularly noises or any form of electrical machinery, since the vibrations created by electrical motors can seriously interfere with the experiment. Clothing should be light and loose, the room should be neither too hot nor too cold, nor too bright or too dark. Outdoors would serve also, provided the questioner lives in a moderate climate and the area in which the experiment is to take place is sufficiently removed from sources of noise or distractions. The experiment may be undertaken alone or in the presence of an observer. But if another person is present, the experimenter should be well acquainted with such person so that no tension, whether conscious or unconscious, arise and cause difficulties in going deeper into self.

Regular breathing, perhaps of the yoga variety, should commence the experiment. After two or three minutes of breathing and perhaps stretching exercises, the physical body of the experimenter should be sufficiently relaxed to permit the state of "suspension" so very necessary for the delving into the past. Next comes a visualization, which must be carried out with as much discipline as the individual is able to muster. In this visualization, all external sources of thought, all memories of the day just past or of external interests must be rigorously excluded. This is not as easy as it sounds. But once one has gotten used to the idea of "chasing one's thoughts" away when they are not wanted or are intruding, the disciplined way toward visualization can be trod without further worry. Visualize yourself now in your present incarnation, as you are now, but in a state of repose, contemplating yourself as a satisfied and balanced individual in full harmony with your surroundings. Even if this is not entirely true, your visualization should suggest it for purposes of going deeper into self.

Since auto-hypnosis and especially regression are impossible for an individual by himself, and attempts of this kind are extremely dangerous, full consciousness must be maintained during these experiments at all times.

The subject should now visualize himself becoming younger and younger and eventually crossing the threshold of birth. A brief moment of reflection as baby should suffice, followed by a visualization of nothingness, of space, or darkness or light, whichever way one is inclined to express the period of transition. This should be followed by the projection of a former self. The thoughts accompanying this mental projection are to be merely of a general suggestive nature, such as, this is what I was before. If the experiment is a success, and it may take several attempts at it to succeed, the subject will in his mind's eye see another person, seemingly occupying the same spacial area as his present physical self. It will take practice and patience to obtain these delicate and sometimes very fleeting impressions of former lives, especially as the present consciousness must be maintained at the same time. But if the experiment is undertaken at regular intervals, bits and pieces of previous existences will in time emerge. It is wise to write them down immediately upon receiving them, or as soon after the experiment as possible. Even though some of this material may stay in the consciousness after the experiment, and become, in fact, part of the waking knowledge of previous lives, the freshness of the immediate impression cannot be overrated.

Begin each session with the unspoken query "Who was I before?" Visualizations will follow, and as you continue with the experiment, more and more details will emerge. Everybody has been through previous lives, with the exception of the new souls, as I have already pointed out. The majority of people undertaking this experiment will therefore experience some sort of projection from past lives and past situations with which they are unfamiliar in their present circumstances. The proof of the pudding lies in these differences, the amount of unfamiliar information, words, descriptions, and other details coming up into the consciousness of the experimenter, which can be checked out for veracity afterwards and judged accordingly as to whether it stems from an alien source. That will be the only proof the individual has that he is not fantasizing; knowledge

150

not contained in his mind, whether conscious or unconscious, knowledge that is reasonably detailed and capable of verification in proper sources is likely to be reincarnation material. In this respect the experimenter should be alert for even the smallest detail, even the tiniest bit of information, whether it "sounds silly" or not, whether it makes any sense to him at the time of reception or not. When delving into possible past lives, the subject is only a recorder and not an editor, consequently any judging or evaluating of the material while it is being dredged up from the past would be detrimental to the outcome and must be avoided at all costs.

False life readers like to impress their clients with the importance of some of the previous lives they have allegedly "discovered" for them. There are dozens of "reborn" Marie Antoinettes, Cleopatras, Julius Caesars, Napoleons, and lesser figures of history. Proof of identity is particularly difficult when we are dealing with well-known historical personalities, but it can be had, and the scientific evidence supporting such a claim would be of the kind that no doubt could exist. On the other hand, previous lives would inevitably involve some knowledge of historical personalities and conditions. Again, the proof lies in the degree of knowledge, in the private details of the material and the general ring of truth to such information. The question is not whether the historical information is accessible in history books and other research sources, but whether the individual concerned would have had access to these sources, and whether the individual having some recall of this kind had *actually consulted* these sources. Thus, the detailed historical knowledge coming from a professional historian would have to be judged quite differently from identical material coming from an illiterate farmer. Information and individual must be weighed very carefully in relation to each other, and the relative inaccessibility of the sources of information also taken into account.

But despite conscious efforts to find out who you were by

151

planning regular experiments, meditation sessions, in which you delve into your potential past lives, there will be many who cannot succeed in this manner. For those there remains only the chance meeting with a person they think they have known before, or a place where they think they've been in the past. These occurrences serve as triggers to jolt their submerged memories, and frequently start a chain of reincarnation flashes as a consequence. But they cannot be induced, nor is there any way in which one can guess at areas where such triggering events may occur. On the other hand, if these unexpected triggers of memory happen, individuals should consider the possibility of hypnotic regression. Under these circumstances, regression might yield much valuable information and possibly provide the rest of the reincarnation memory.

Each lifetime leaves an imprint in the soul of the individual, so that at the end of a number of incarnations the sum total of earlier incarnations also remains within the personality. Some element in the past is absorbed into the next stage and so on, thus shaping an old soul from many layers, many experiences of different kinds. One lifetime does not only serve as springboard for the next, in that the Karmic Law adjusts the mistake of the earlier existence in the next one, but it supplies the individual with "personality substance" which can be utilized in subsequent incarnations. Frequently, individuals find that they can do certain things surprisingly well, or are able to grasp ideas, teachings, techniques as if they had somehow been taught them before and this forgotten knowledge was merely being reawakened in them in their present incarnation. In such cases they are indeed drawing upon the deeper, earlier layers of their individual consciousness. The feelings of previous knowledge are not strong enough to be considered separate reincarnation memories. But they are nevertheless useful in developing certain skills, when these skills coincide with something one has learned in an earlier incarnation. *Each lifetime is not an experience unto itself, but, just as the rings of an aging tree, contribute to the building of the overall soul.* Man is the sum total of all of his incarnations on the earth plane, taking with him to the next stage of existence all that which he has learned from each individual incarnation. Nothing is lost, nothing was in vain; everything builds towards a fuller and more complete, a more harmonious and therefore a more perfect individual.

Chapter 12
The Ultimate Goal

Those who are opposed to the philosophy based upon reincarnation confess that they see no real purpose, no real goal in such a system. What is the point, they argue, to be born again and again, to make the same mistakes, or at best to improve a little upon previous performance, when all this effort could be put to better use in one single lifetime? Such critics also fail to understand the need for forgetfulness from one incarnation to the next, except in special cases. I have already pointed out that the material known to me suggesting reincarnation also involves previous lives cut short by a variety of circumstances. I have pointed out that the overwhelming majority of reincarnation memories includes death by violence or in suffering, premature death, unfinished business, incomplete missions, and other forms of disrupted activities. It would therefore appear that the "bonus" of limited memories is a way by which the Karmic Law compensates an individual for shortcomings in a previous lifetime. The additional knowledge of the problems of the previous incarnation helps the individual make decisions with a greater degree of insight in the next one. As a result, harmony and balance are restored once again. If everyone knew the details of his previous life on earth, there would be no point in having free will, for one thing. With such foreknowledge, everybody could then do "the right thing" next time around, having profited from his past mistakes. No special effort would be required for this; to the contrary, knowledge of errors in past lives would tend to lessen the desire to put forth any effort in the next one.

But man has a right to ask, where does the system lead, what is the ultimate purpose and what is the maximum accomplishment, the desired end product? To leave such matters entirely to the deity, or to the interpretors of the deity, the priests, rabbis, ministers, and on earth, is to be less than a responsible human being. *For if man is a creation in the image of the deity, he has not only the right but the sacred duty to inform himself of his purpose; he must become aware of his destiny in order to fulfill it.*

Scientifically speaking, the evidence for reincarnation is very strong, convincing in a large number of cases, where alternate explanations will not suffice. But we do not know whether reincarnation occurs in every case, to every human being, from the beginning of time, and how many times man reincarnates. We assume, by deduction, that reincarnation holds true for all mankind. This seems a logical conclusion based upon the fact that natural law works equally for all life in the universe.

We are on less certain grounds when it comes to the number of reincarnations required of or possible for each human being. Indian philosophy has long held that reincarnation is governed by astrological cycles. The number of required reincarnations are twelve, one under each sign of the Zodiac. Beyond that, Indian philosophy holds, individuals may elect to return for additional incarnations, but are not required to do so under the law. There is nothing scientifically evidential in this assumption. If anything, the evidence seems to point in other directions. For example, there are cases where valid reincarnation memories involve a previous life under the identical Zodiac sign as the present one, not merely one in twelve. Of course, we have no way of proving that twelve is the number of required incarnations. Possibly, if the Indian philosophical concept is true, each soul must go through the twelve signs of the Zodiac at least *once*, although it may go through repetitions of birth signs in addition.

Also part of the Eastern philosophy, especially the Indian, is the concept of Nirvana. This is the ultimate state of being, in which the individual becomes part of the Godhead. At the point of entering Nirvana the individual loses all individuality, gives up the ego, and submerges itself in the fountainhead, the original source whence it came. The concept of Nirvana is basically alien to Western thinking. Westerners like to believe in individual consciousness and the survival of individual personality. Easterners lean towards a cessation of individual personality in favor of becoming part of a single world mind or deity concept. Perhaps the different approach is due to the nature of East and West, West being more action-minded in its religious concepts, East being the more passive world. To the majority of Westerners, entering Nirvana is a copout; to the Easterner, it is utmost fulfillment. Materialists relish the thought of oblivion at the moment of physical death. Such concepts help them live a life of total selfishness, without regard for post-mortem existence or reckoning. Strange as it may seem, spiritualists also look askance at reincarnation concepts which make the soul come back to the earth sphere time and again. For many years, all evidential material pointing towards reincarnation was arbitrarily suppressed by the spiritualist press. In this respect spiritualism acted no different from any orthodox religion which ignored that which it could not work into its own dogmatic system. In recent years, however, spiritualism has become more tolerant towards the concept of reincarnation. It still doesn't know how it can reconcile its own tenets with the concept that man returns time and again. To the spiritualist, evidence of reincarnation memories are better explained as communication between a discarnate soul and a living one in which the person from the past uses the person in the present to communicate and express himself, perhaps air suppressed grievances and otherwise live again second-hand. When this becomes dramatically or oppressive traumatic, spiritualists speak of possession. But the evidence for personal reincarnation is much too voluminous, much too convincing, to be brushed aside in favor of a naive spiritualist philosophy.

Actually, there is *no conflict* between the concept of religious spiritualism and reincarnation evidence. Where spiritualists present evidence of communication with deceased individuals who lived during the past few hundred years, the evidence seems very valid and well supported. However, whenever spiritualists come up with alleged communications from individuals having lived thousands of years ago, possibly in strange and exotic lands. These communications lack the ring of truth and the supporting evidence which seems so plentiful in earlier periods of history.

This makes me wonder whether spiritualists are not perhaps dealing with two separate sets of circumstances: the evidential material of their communications with discarnates is proof of the existence of another dimension, the next dimension in fact, where discarnates live on after physical death. But after a certain period of time, varying greatly between just a few years and several centuries and according to needs, these discarnates disappear from that sphere and return to physical life as reincarnated individuals. I find that whenever some Master or special guide is quoted, such personalities are not capable of historical verification. Too little is being said about them, their names, circumstances and other details of their lives in the past which could be checked out. This does not disprove their existence, to be sure. It is theoretically possible that an individual goes through the required number of incarnations, and at the end reverts to one chosen lifetime, dwelling in the highest spheres from then on in and acting as Master or guide to those on the earth plane. But such claims are very difficult to prove in purely scientific terms. It might be well to study such interesting works as Anthony Borgia's three books dealing with life after death, published in England. Borgia's communicator, a Roman Catholic Monsignor, speaks of a number of spheres, one higher than the next, and maintains that the world beyond this one is made up of a succession of spheres. There are reports of encounters with beings from the higher dimensions. Some of the passages in Borgia's books remind one of similar descriptions given by Emanuel Swedenborg. Whatever the validity of his statements, it seems certain that the world beyond the physical one is by no means a homogeneous entity, but consists of various layers of consciousness.

When it comes to the so-called Masters, we are entering the realms of metaphysics. Masters or guides, sometimes called controls, are superior human beings who live in the spiritual world but help guide the lives of those in the physical world. Many deep trance mediums have such controls, some have not. Most of the philosophical concepts of the East rely upon wisdom from the Masters to sustain those on earth. Masters turn up who were at one time people living useful lives on earth, who have progressed to the status of teacher. The difficulty in differentiating between real Masters, who once lived on earth, no matter how long ago and no matter where, and the fanciful creations of some individuals requiring the crutch of a superior guide, is a very real one: ultimately, the proof lies in pinpointing the earthly existence of the alleged Master. To many, this seems neither necessary nor even desirable. They feel that the message is the thing; what does it matter if the Master cannot be traced, or his existence proven, if the words coming from him are of such great impact? There is a grain of truth in such attitudes, because the message is, after all, the thing. But it would be comforting to know whether a guiding principle or message of wisdom comes from within oneself or from some exterior and wiser source.

I do not doubt in the least that there are superior beings, whether they are termed Masters or guides, whose task it is to intervene in human affairs to the extent that natural law allows them. Frequently, they manipulate natural law in such a way that certain chains of events take place, never once breaking, breaching or circumventing natural law in the process. In some cases, where the recipient is an advanced soul, direct contact between Master and guided individual takes place. I have written of such an instance in *Born Again,* when reporting the amazing material received by Alice McDermott from the late philosopher-painter Nicholas Roerich.

Evidence that further lifetimes are spent on other planets of our solar system is totally wanting, except in unsupported statements from some metaphysically inclined individuals. Evidence that souls from other galaxies incarnate in ours is equally absent. What it comes down to, in the end, is that we are a self-contained world, whether on the physical plane or on the higher levels. This does not preclude that similar systems exist in other galaxies, to the contrary, it is highly likely that the universe consists of parallel systems of this nature. But as long as we proceed along the cautious, scientific path, no matter how open-mindedly, we must reject the notion that souls pierce the space barrier at will, and that superior wisdom from other worlds, physically speaking, is penetrating ours. If it is, it must come from space travelers in *material* vehicles.

It seems far more likely that the energy fields called human personality, which are similar in structure but unique in terms of specifics, keep being reused time and again. Energy does dissipate, but at such a slow pace that it would appear very remote in terms of our time-space continuum. It would seem to follow that reincarnation occurs, in each case, until the energy potential has been used up. At that point new souls would have to be created from the universal reservoir. Since the moment when the individual energy field is fully dissipated is a very remote one, it would stand to reason that a large number of reincarnations would take place until that point is reached. It does therefore not seem very likely that the East Indian philosophical concept of twelve reincarnations to coincide with the twelve signs of the Zodiac can be supported by the evidence, both by the present evidence and by knowledge to be gained in the future. It may well be that the idea of twelve signs of the Zodiac concerns the minimum of required incarnations, in which case they represent not a scientific fact but a religious concept.

No other explanation fits the facts of human life as clearly and as widely as does reincarnation. The inequities of our lives would be senseless and illogical unless some deeper meaning lay underneath them, and unless life extended beyond one life span for each individual. Only in terms of a higher point of view would such injustices and hardships be acceptable. If we are to reject the concept of reincarnation and force the facts at hand to be contained in a single lifetime, then we would, by necessity, have to invent a revengeful deity, whose punishments these hardships represent.

In order to make them plausible, however, we would have to allow for a variety of sins and transgressions, many of which are committed unknowingly. But that is not enough. In order to account for all the bad things happening to humanity on earth, sins, omissions, and transgressions would have to be invented which aren't really sins at all when viewed from the point of view of natural law. They become sin only if they are measured against man-made dogmatic concepts, man-made religions, and man-made morality. We would then construct our own cage, putting into it wild beasts of our own creation, when we accept a one-lifetime-only concept.

Everything in nature dies and is reborn; one need only observe the trees and plants, one need only study the cycles of life, the patterns of birth, death and rebirth, *to realize that man cannot be altogether different from the rest of the universe.* We, too, die and are reborn, regularly, and according to a definite system, and it is in this cycle of birth, death and rebirth, that our growth lies.

For man to live a perfect life in harmony with his environment, he need only be conscious of these facts. Adjusting his everyday activities and both his thoughts and actions to a wider view of the universe, he will learn to live in tune with nature, and in tune with the rise and fall of the forces in nature, and no longer spend valuable energies opposing them.

Everything that happens must be viewed in terms of usefulness not only to self but to others and to the environment as a whole. Everything that happens to a person must be looked at in terms of a possible link with another human being and of a deeper purpose behind it. *Nothing in nature must be considered chance or coincidence.* Life is not a haphazard accident on a tiny planet in a remote section of the Milky Way. It is a well-planned, well-executed manifestation of a superior will and power, and even though we may only hold a tiny fraction of the truth in our consciousness, we are capable of eventually grasping the rest of it.

The patterns of destiny are laid out well in advance of our coming by the administrators of the Karmic Law, which is part

162

of the universal law under which all that exists operates. The patterns oblige us only to react to them whenever we come in contact with their highlights. They do not dictate our decisions. But superior knowledge of the patterns and the meaning of our individual destinies will help us make the right decisions at the right time. It is also well to keep in mind that there is neither beginning nor end, only motion. In moving forward from one incarnation to the next, we are developing the inheritance given us at the beginning of our conscious existence. At the highest point lies not descent, but greater and even greater tasks up ahead. For in a dimensionless world thought itself becomes manifest destiny. Even if we do not wish to aim that high, our journey along the so-called time track will be a more enjoyable, a more useful one, and a safer trip, if we are constantly aware of the *Patterns of Destiny* that surround us. For beyond destiny lies nothingness.